CW01095585

'Paul Watts brings a life-time's
as he shares with the reader thi
church he has so lovingly serv
are intertwined in a pastoral na
particular part of the Lord's harvest field.

The bookshops are groaning with secular handbooks on managing change, but Watts is right to remind us that change has a purpose, and that this purpose is bound up in the glory of God. The challenges laid out here, of navigating gospel-driven change in a God-glorifying way, will give food for thought to pastors and congregations alike, whatever the specifics of their pastoral position or particular struggle.

This delightful account of a gospel ministry is realistic about the difficulties and disappointments a church must face but, because it is rooted firmly in the riches of the gospel, it is an encouraging tale that is full of hope and joy. I am certain that the reader will find hope for their heart, and joy in their soul, as they reflect with the author on how to trust God and serve him forever wherever the Lord has placed us.'

Revd Mark Wallace, St Peter's Church, Colchester

'I loved reading this book. I have had a keen interest in this gospel work in Coventry over many years. It has had a major impact on my own outlook for good. I am pleased to have in print what God has done and taught them. The principles and practical wisdom in this book are not limited to Coventry, however. All those wrestling with handling change in a way that is biblical, wise, loving, sensitive and faithful will find help in its pages. Hopefully that includes most of us!'

John Cowley, Pastor, Forest Fold Baptist Church, Crowborough, East Sussex

'This book contains a feast of good things. I was delighted to read it and am pleased to give it a hearty endorsement. It is at one and the same time, the very engaging story of a church faced with the need to remain faithful to its heritage and also meet the challenge of changing times, and the story of the way its pastor and other elders faced these challenges, in dependence on God. The book is particularly helpful because all the way through, it is clear that thirty years of gospel-driven change were won through by dependence on a spirit of prayer and a willingness to seek the mind of God through his Word. I am very pleased to commend this book and hope it enjoys a wide readership.'

Phil Arthur, retired pastor of Grace Baptist Church, Lancaster

'Navigating change has become one of the biggest challenges in life for our generation. This is true for everyone in our rapidly changing world, but it presents its own unique challenge for Christians and what it means for the church and all too often has led to lessons being learned the hard way.

Paul Watts' delightfully engaging book addresses this issue in a way that will surely resonate with Christians and churches on multiple levels. He doesn't simply offer yet another manual for handling change in the church. Instead, he tells the story of the congregation he has belonged to and served for most of his life and teases out the Bible truths and principles that brought them through to where they are today.

He rightly points out that change for its own sake is never a good thing. However, as we grasp the glory of the gospel – what it is, who it is for and where it ultimately brings us – then we will begin to see the necessity of the right kind of change as it does its work in us and through us.

This is indeed a book for our times and one that many will wish had been available years ago. It is certain to be a huge help and encouragement to Christians everywhere.'

Mark G. Johnston, Trinity Church EP, Richhill, Co. Armagh

'There is nothing ordinary about the glory of God, but his glory is often put on display in what seems to be very ordinary. In a humble and unassuming way Paul shares the story of how the glorious unchanging gospel of our Lord Jesus Christ brought about gradual change in an ordinary local church and in the lives of men and women. It is a reminder that change is at the heart of the gospel and that we should both expect it and welcome it. A delightful book to encourage servants of our Lord Jesus to trust God to do what is extraordinary, through what may look very ordinary.'

Jonathan Prime, Head of local ministries, FIEC

GOSPEL-DRIVEN
CHANGE

GOSPEL-DRIVEN
CHANGE

NAVIGATING REFORM IN A LOCAL CHURCH

PAUL WATTS

Grace
Publications

Grace Publications Trust
www.gracepublications.co.uk

First published in Great Britain by Grace Publications Trust 2022

Cover design by Pete Barnsley (CreativeHoot.com)

ISBN: 978-1-91215442-5

Printed and bound in Great Britain by Clays Ltd, Elcograf S.p.A.

'I do it all for the sake of the gospel' – 1 Corinthians 9:23

To my lovely wife, Hazel, who has been at my side every step of this journey we have shared together – Genesis 2:18

Contents

Foreword

Bill and Sharon James

When we moved to Leamington Spa to start ministry at Emmanuel Church in 1991, Rehoboth Church in Coventry was a rather forbidding Strict Baptist Chapel. Bill was invited to preach in 1996 and was faced with rows of pews occupied by a congregation in formal dress, complete with hats for the ladies. He had to select hymns from *Gadsby's Hymnbook*, and was rather anxious about offending this traditional congregation.

Appearances can be deceptive. For all of the evident formality, this was a friendly and warm-hearted people. Over the years, this church would become for us a home-from-home, where we would often attend when on holiday from Emmanuel. We were privileged to witness the church's transformation as it emerged from its Gospel Standard roots to become a welcoming and vibrant multi-ethnic congregation. The layout of the building was transformed, and ultimately rebuilt from the inside out. Partnership with a local Baptist church developed into a merger, desiring to reach this deprived inner-city area more effectively with the gospel. The old church name Rehoboth, while held in great affection, was given up to become Lower Ford Street Baptist as a reflection of their commitment to the local area. Ultimately the church family would adopt the name of their sister church and local area Hillfields.

The Lord was clearly at work in such radical transformation, peacefully effected. The human instruments of this change were Paul and Hazel Watts. Paul's own background in Gospel Standard circles gave him a sympathy and understanding of the people. His faithful and warm-hearted biblical preaching was the means used by the Spirit to change hearts and minds. His patient and wise leadership over the years, alongside his fellow elder Peter Cordle and his wife, Janet, enabled the church family to move forwards step by step.

When local pastors formed the Coventry Evangelical Fellowship as a fraternal and means of co-operation and fellowship between churches in the area, Paul was the obvious candidate to assume leadership. From that time Bill referred to Paul as the 'Bishop of Coventry'! Behind the teasing was acknowledgement of the honour and respect in which he was held.

We are delighted that Paul has now provided this record of what the Lord has done over the years in and through this local church family. It is a great encouragement to read as a history of the Lord's goodness and a model of humble and faithful biblical leadership, which provides lessons for us all.

Preface

Change can be stressful in any department of life. A house move brings upheaval. A change of job calls for new skills and adjustment to a different team. A change of opinion can result in loss of face or friendship. The negative dimensions of change are often those that most capture our attention. Intuitively we get the connection in the old hymn between 'change and decay'.[1]

At the same time, we all recognise that change is often necessary, and for the better. An achievement, a promotion, a new situation in life can be wonderfully exhilarating. 'Progress' has a gloss that 'change' lacks. 'Reformation' also suggests change with a shine on it.

Whether we welcome or resist it, we all know that change is inevitable. Negotiating it is a life skill. In facing up to change, lessons are learned that we might otherwise miss. Obstacles are overcome. Progress is made.

The subject of this book is navigating change in the local

---

1   'Change and decay in all around I see' from 'Abide with me, fast falls the eventide', Henry Francis Lyte, 1793-1847.

church. For Christians, local church life is our main way of living out, with others, what it means to be a Christian. A biblical understanding of its significance brings it to the centre of our lives. We invest into it, rightly, with spiritual and emotional intensity.

For this reason alone, change in this sphere can be particularly difficult to handle. Our first response is often at an emotional level. We see ourselves as the victims of change, or as resistance fighters against it. At best, we brand ourselves survivors. Few of us are genuine pioneers, grasping change eagerly. Most are inherently cautious. We often expect change in the local church to be more painful and disorientating than exciting and fruitful. Yet we can probably all look back on changes that have taken place in church life, only to admit that they were for the best. Advance in the kingdom of God is the theme of many of Jesus' parables. A mustard seed has a disproportionate potential for growth (Mk. 4:30–32).

My case in these pages is that, while change is by no means positive per se, and change for change's sake is definitely suspect, change for the sake of the gospel is authentic. Are there ways of discerning what change needs to take place in the local church for the gospel's sake? Are there ways of managing it well and navigating it skilfully?

Resistance to change is, after all, in some ways a strange phenomenon among Christians. The gospel is about change. Regeneration, repentance and faith in Christ, produces profound, personal change. Jesus spoke of it in these terms, 'Truly, truly, I say to you, unless a grain of wheat falls into the ground and dies, it remains alone; but if it dies it bears much fruit' (Jn. 12:24).

When a person forgives, and is reconciled to another, for example, something has changed. When the apostle Peter exhorts believers to 'grow in the grace and knowledge of our Lord Jesus Christ', he is clearly expecting us to change (2 Pet. 3:18). Such personal advance in the Christian life is costly, but worth it. After all, the ultimate Christian hope is that 'we shall be changed' (1 Cor. 15:51–52). There will be a new heaven and a new earth. Our natural resistance to this sanctifying kind of change is part of our fallen human nature.

We might think it sensible for Christians instinctively to be suspicious of changes that occur in the world around us. This also needs proper discrimination. While it is prudent to be cautious, it is also wise to be ready to adapt. We must learn to speak into such change, and to use it, otherwise we slip into irrelevance, get stuck in a time warp, enclose ourselves in a ghetto. When Christians find themselves preaching only to the converted, it is a disaster.

Some developments in the outside world actually prove advantageous to the spread of the gospel. Think of the invention of the printing press just in time for the Protestant Reformation. Parallels can be made with the current digital revolution, providing new, far-reaching conduits for the gospel message to a global audience. Changes in technology and their social consequences are by no means all bad.

Likewise, not all change in church life is harmful. Just as change in nature can be a sign of life, so also it can be in grace. When individual believers grow in likeness to Jesus, such growth will change them. If all the believers in a local church are thus being transformed from one degree of glory to another (2 Cor. 3:18), the church itself will be changing – in the love of its members for one another, in practical care for the weak and vulnerable, in compassion for the lost. In other words, visible change will occur at street level.

The first thing to grasp, then, is that some change, like the process of ageing, is inevitable. Social, political and environmental conditions are in constant flux. Technological developments occur at breakneck speed. Events such as the coronavirus pandemic only serve to accelerate the pace. Some of the changes spawned are irreversible.

All this is bound to impact the way we 'do' church. Changing conditions necessitate a rethink. Those who try to hold on to doing things the way they have always been done, are historically inaccurate. They have not always been done that way. There was a time, for example, when the singing of hymns in English independent churches was an innovation. Was it a good one? Every generation must assess and reassess. The change, as it occurred, had to be managed carefully – as all change must. In some churches they had, for a while, only one hymn right at the end of the service, so that those who disagreed with hymn singing could withdraw.

For forty-five years, my wife, Hazel, and I have been members of a church in Coventry. For thirty-five of those years, I was its pastor, more recently joined by other pastoral colleagues. For reasons that will become apparent, this is a church that over that time has experienced more change than most. It has emerged – is emerging – from a quite distinctive Christian subculture. Some readers will instantly recognise the scene. To others, from other church backgrounds, aspects of it will be unfamiliar. Head coverings for women may never have been an issue in your church. Nonetheless, there are likely to be issues in your context that, in a parallel way, pose significant challenges for navigating change. It may be, for example, that a white middle-class undercurrent of criticism about other people's lack of punctuality could helpfully be addressed where you are placed.

The nine chapters of this book are divided into two sections. Chapters 1 to 6 take the recent history of our church in Hillfields, Coventry, as a case study. This is not offered as a model, nor are the changes that have occurred presented as recommendations. Rather, my hope is that our story will illustrate the challenges, struggles and mistakes, as well as the minor triumphs, that can occur when gospel-driven change is put in place. The way this is navigated in one church, and the biblical principles applied, may be of significant help to another in a very different context.

Chapter 6, in this first section, entitled 'Slices of Life', adds human colour to the story, giving glimpses into some of the more quirky aspects of a pastor's life over a long ministry. The gospel always comes to individuals – and individual people are endlessly interesting!

Chapters 7 to 9, the second section of the book, then attempt to distil some of the lessons we have learned with reference to biblical principles and practice in the field. Our experience in Coventry, including the jolt of ejection from our denomination, can stimulate thought, prayer and action among other church people and leaders. Like us, you may be struggling with change, but see that it must come if the gospel is to run freely and effectively in an ever-changing culture (2 Thess. 3:1). Pastors, elders and church leaders, especially, need a lot of wisdom and grace, not to say grit and courage, to navigate such change. We need to gain the trust of the people we serve. We need to lead by example. We need to focus attention on issues of substance rather than style. We need to achieve both cultural relevance and continuity. We need to take the people with us. Above all, we need the wisdom that comes from above (Jas. 1:5–6).

At the same time, congregations facing change need to hold realistic expectations and to be prayerfully supportive of their leaders, neither campaigning constantly for pet ideas nor resisting all change on principle. My aim in the following pages is to help Christians across a variety of church contexts. At the heart of my approach is an essential test for any proposed change: is it, or is it not, for the sake of the gospel?

Before we attend to these things, however, we must lay a foundation to demonstrate the great cultural hospitality of the gospel itself.

Introduction:
The gospel crosses cultures

The gospel itself does not change. The historic, apostolic gospel of God's free and sovereign grace is powerfully, succinctly defined by the apostle Paul by the inspiration of the Holy Spirit:

> Now I would remind you ... of the gospel I preached to you, which you received, in which you stand, and by which you are being saved, if you hold fast to the word I preached to you – unless you believed in vain. For I delivered to you as of first importance what I also received: that Christ died for our sins in accordance with the Scriptures, that he was buried, that he was raised on the third day in accordance with the Scriptures, and that he appeared to Cephas, then to the twelve (1 Cor. 15:1-5).

This is the irreducible, non-negotiable, unchanging gospel of the grace of God. It is clear from the early Christian preaching, immediately recoverable from the Acts of the Apostles, that a distinct message was heralded: the proclamation of the death, burial and resurrection, ascension, exaltation and return of Jesus Christ. The first hearers of this good news were charged with either being complicit in the rejection and crucifixion of the Son of God (Acts 2) or with being ignorant of God (Acts 17). Newly convicted of their sin, they were called upon to repent and receive the good news of the free forgiveness of sins through faith in Christ.

It is also clear from the whole New Testament, especially the letters of Paul, that the early church – quickly and radically forming and spreading as the gospel was declared – was confessional. It not only had a distinct message but a definite creed and theology, 'the whole counsel of God', based on all of Scripture, and fully centred on the person and work of Jesus Christ (Acts 20:27). To change this message, or its authentic theological constructs, is to depart from Christian orthodoxy and faithfulness.

Our twenty-first-century world bears some striking resemblances to the world of the first century, when the gospel was first unleashed in the full glory of its revelation. People today are often open, as then, to various forms of spirituality. A common language, Greek, then facilitated the spread of the gospel throughout the known world. In a similar way, technology enables global communication today. There are, of course, dramatic differences, but the need in both centuries is the same. The world in every age needs the gospel above all else. For a church, or preacher, to go off-message, under the pressure to entertain or accommodate to the culture is a terrible betrayal. To dilute the gospel is to deprive the world of the very message it most needs.

The Bible

If the gospel does not change, neither does the Bible in which
it is rooted. Orthodox mainstream Christianity is biblical
Christianity. The Bible in its original manuscripts in Hebrew
and Greek, in all its sixty-six canonical books, is the inspired,
inerrant, infallible Word of God. 'All Scripture is breathed out by
God, and is profitable for teaching, for reproof, for correction,
and for training in righteousness, that the man of God may be
complete, equipped for every good work' (2 Tim. 3:16-17). This
is the only ultimate authority, under Christ himself, for what
the Christian church believes and practices. It is sufficient. It
is not Bible plus tradition, or experience, or creeds, or church,
but *sola scriptura* (Scripture alone).

An apostolic push

One of the events in the Winter Olympics is an ice-skating
relay. But how do you pass on the baton on ice? You come up
behind the next 'runner' and give him a push to send him on his
way. Towards the end of the New Testament (in 2 Timothy) we
witness an apostolic push. The great apostle Paul has almost
finished his race. He has travelled the world, preached the
gospel, planted churches, appointed elders, written letters,
and suffered appalling privation. Now he is ready to depart
to be with Christ. As he writes to a young apostolic delegate,
Timothy, he makes it abundantly clear that what has been
his priority is also to be Timothy's: to preach the Word. Paul
gives Timothy a solemn charge, 'in the presence of God and of

Christ Jesus, who is to judge the living and the dead' (2 Tim. 4:1). Whatever the current conditions of receptivity or otherwise in the world, he must preach the gospel 'in season and out of season' (2 Tim. 4:2). Any local church, truly committed to the Bible and the gospel, must do the same.

Roots in Judaism

The roots of the Christian church and its gospel go down deep into Judaism. Jesus himself was a Jew. All his immediate twelve disciples were Jews, though there was significant diversity in their social background and political outlook within Judaism. Simon the Zealot was a different kind of Jew from Matthew the tax-collector: one a political radical and activist, wanting to resist the Roman occupation with every fibre of his being; the other a collaborator with the Romans. Sparks could fly between these two, and probably did!

Just so, in the church today we must expect people of different social backgrounds and political outlooks – people who voted for Brexit, along with those who voted Remain. Were there more working men than intellectuals among the disciples Jesus chose? The diversity of their personalities is striking – impetuous Peter; James and John the sons of thunder; Andrew the people-person; Thomas, the pessimist (every church has at least one!).

For all this diversity, the very early church was a Jewish church, holding to the food laws, observing the Sabbath, still worshipping in the Jerusalem temple. The Acts of the Apostles begins with one hundred and twenty Jewish Christians, though not known as yet by the name Christian (Acts 11:26). Even on the Day of Pentecost the three thousand converts were all Jews, most of them pilgrim diaspora Jews, their homes scattered through the empire, where they lived cheek by jowl with Gentiles, speaking their language, knowing their culture.

Growing diversity

The diversity in the church was growing and the Hellenistic Jews were to become a vital bridgehead in the God-ordained campaign to transpose the gospel into the Gentile world. Stephen the Hellenistic Jew, and first Christian martyr, paved the way by his radical preaching (Acts 7), while Peter, the Galilean Jew, had his cultural and theological presuppositions turned upside down as the Holy Spirit guided him unmistakeably to preach the gospel to a Roman centurion (Acts 10).

The Acts of the Apostles, telling how the good news went from Jerusalem to Rome, is a story of profound, gospel-driven change. A relatively small community faced a massive influx. A predominantly Jewish Christian church had to learn how to absorb Gentile converts. For the people who lived through it, it was not comfortable. Almost every cherished social norm and cultural presupposition went into the melting pot. The radical conclusion of the whole story would soon be, 'There is neither Jew nor Greek, there is neither slave nor free, there is neither male nor female: for you are all one in Christ Jesus' (Gal. 3:28).

We might find it natural to suppose that it must have been easier for them. After all, they had the exceptional, powerful work and influence of the Holy Spirit poured out at Pentecost to propel them through all this change. They had the power not of positive thinking but of God. They had no buildings, no organised campaigns, no trained ministry, no theological colleges but 'with great power the apostles gave witness to the resurrection of the Lord Jesus, and great grace was upon them all' (Acts 4:33).

Yet this power did not mean that the changes they faced were less real and, at points, less painful. They needed always to be a praying church, to 'devote themselves to the apostles' doctrine and fellowship, to the breaking of bread and prayers' (Acts 2:42). They needed definite gospel intent. They did not have a church growth manual. But they did have purpose and out of that purpose grew strategies. They shared their possessions, they submitted their lifestyle to the gospel, they met together regularly, they had recognised leaders. They were a visible, purposeful community of God's people. At their best, they had only one agenda – to do the will of Jesus Christ, the great Head of the Church.

In all these respects, the same is true for the church today. The empowerment of the Holy Spirit may not manifest itself to us in just the same way as among the first Christians, but we do still have the very same Holy Spirit, the same resource, the same promises. Equipped by him, we must navigate gospel-driven change as they did. If they needed the courage of gospel ambition, so do we. If they needed to cross cultural boundaries with the good news, so do we. If they were absolutely dependent on the Holy Spirit, so are we.

In the period covered by the Acts of the Apostles, Judaism was to some extent still a protected, lawful religion within the Roman Empire. It was allowed to conduct its own religious affairs. While the followers of 'the Way' were identified by the Romans as a sect within Judaism (Acts 9:2), they were reasonably safeguarded. The story of Acts is an ejection story. Hostility against the Way was almost always first stirred up by Jewish people. As the brothers of Joseph threw him out, so now their descendants ejected the followers of Jesus. At the end of Acts, the Romans are still acting as uneasy protectors of the new religion, but the situation is becoming increasingly dangerous and fragile.

It became clear apostolic policy to preach the gospel first in the synagogues, to Jews; then, upon rejection, to turn to the Gentiles (Acts 13:46–48). The church of Jesus Christ was gradually emerging as a new, separate, evangelistic, culturally hospitable community. Led and inspired by the Holy Spirit they crossed new frontiers. Barriers were broken down. Samaritans were evangelised. An African official was converted. A Roman centurion and his household were baptised. The questions became ever more urgent: 'Can the church of Jesus Christ receive Gentile converts and remain one church? Can a Gentile male join the new Israel of God without being circumcised?'

It is perhaps difficult for those of us who are Gentiles today, and who hold many Gentile presuppositions about the church, to realise how deep the cultural issues were in the early church. The Council of Jerusalem was a defining moment (Acts 15). Its conclusions were a radical compromise to allow cultural and religious adaptation. It is the backstory of so many of the New Testament writings. Paul famously expresses his personal adaptability for the sake of the gospel:

> to the Jews I became as a Jew, in order to win Jews. To those under the law I became as one under the law (though not being myself under the law) that I may win those under the law. To those outside the law I became as one outside the law (not being outside the law of God but under the law of Christ) that I might win those outside the law. To the weak I became weak, that I might win the weak. I have become all things to all people, that by all means I might save some. I do it all for the sake of the gospel, that I may share with them in its blessings (1 Cor. 9:20-23).

Humanly speaking, the 'Pharisee of the Pharisees' would never have initiated such accommodation. Neither would a Galilean fisherman. Both Paul and Peter were tested severely on their religious, cultural adaptability. The strain on Peter is shown by the fact that, under the scrutiny of the 'circumcision party', he later reneged on his newfound freedom in Christ (Gal. 1). Only the power of God could overcome such barriers – the power that led Saul of Tarsus to become Paul, the apostle to the Gentiles, who asserted 'one Lord, one faith, one baptism' (Eph. 4:5).

It was always meant to be like this

God chose Abraham and his descendants to be the specific family and nation through which he would achieve his great plan of redemption. Israel was to be a light to the nations. In that sense, God's plans were never ethnocentric. Jacob's family had 'Aramean, Amorite, Canaanite and Egyptian elements within it'.[2] Foreigners were to be welcomed, provided for and integrated. The prohibitions against mixed marriages were more about preserving spiritual than ethnic distinctiveness. Non-Israelites such as Rahab, Ruth and the widow of Zarephath were grafted in. The names of Rahab and Ruth even appear in the genealogy of the Messiah (Matt. 1:5). The message to the non-Israelite stranger was eloquently expressed by Moses to Hobab, 'Come with us and we will do good to you, for the LORD has promised good to Israel' (Num. 10:29).

God is as deeply concerned for all people-groups in the Old Testament as he is in the New. 'The earth is the LORD's and the fullness thereof, the world and those who dwell therein' (Ps. 24:1). The prophet Isaiah declares Israel's calling to be salt and light to the nations:

> the time is coming to gather all nations and tongues. And they shall come and shall see my glory, and I will set a sign among them. And from them I will send survivors to the nations ... to the coastlands far away, that have not heard my fame or seen my glory. And they shall declare my glory among the Gentiles (Isa. 66:18–19).

It is not a surprise, therefore, in the opening pages of the New Testament to find that the Gentile nations, represented by wise men from the East, recognise the Messiah, that the

---

2   J. Daniel Hays, *From Every People and Nation* (Downer's Grove: IVP, 2003), p. 85.

message of the angels is one of joy to all people, and that Simeon prophesies the light of revelation to the Gentiles. Even Galilee, firmly in Jewish territory, yet with a diverse mix, was known as 'Galilee of the Gentiles' (Matt. 4:15). Jesus famously singled out the faith of a Roman Centurion and a Syro-Phonecian woman. His encounter with the woman of Samaria was a sign of the Samaritan mission to come. The way he mixed with despised groups, and broke through cultural and social taboos, was a source of deep perplexity to Jerusalem's religious elite. His ministry, like his apostles after him, was 'to the Jew first', but it was also his clear mandate that his gospel should be proclaimed among the nations, 'They will come from the east and the west, the north and the south and sit down in the Kingdom of God' (Lk. 13:29; cf. Matt. 28:18–20 NKJV). This should produce great celebration and thankfulness among those of us who are Gentiles. We are included!

The vision of heaven in the book of Revelation reflects this diversity:

> After this I looked, and behold, a great multitude that no one could number, from every nation, from all tribes and peoples and languages, standing before the throne and before the Lamb, clothed in white robes, with palm branches in their hands, and crying out with a loud voice, 'Salvation belongs to our God who sits on the throne, and to the Lamb' (Rev. 7:9,10).

We feel instinctively positive about such a glorious eschatological vision. But are we equally enthusiastic about the dismantling of cultural barriers in the church on earth?

We carry more cultural baggage than we think. But should we not always be working towards greater cultural hospitality, expecting the church on earth to reflect at least the same kind of diversity, if not on the same scale, as the church in glory?

Antioch in Syria

Antioch in Syria was a large port city in the Graeco-Roman Empire. People from all over the Mediterranean (Greeks, Romans, Arabs, Syrians, Cappadocians and Jews) did business there. This did not always breed friendship and multi-ethnic harmony; more often the opposite. But the *church* in Antioch became different. It began to learn to welcome people regardless of status, culture or ethnicity. Here was a community where people belonged simply on the basis of repentance towards God and faith in the Lord Jesus Christ. A powerful new prophetic message was being transmitted from church to city.[3]

What happened in Antioch was a kind of eureka moment in the early Christian church (Acts 11:19–26). There are of course other important markers in the story of the gospel moving out from its exclusively Jewish context including: the return of the Pentecost converts to their homes in the Hellenistic world, the scattering of Christians in the persecution following Stephen's martyrdom, the mission led by Philip in Samaria, the conversion of the first African, and Peter preaching to Cornelius in Caesarea.

---

3 This paragraph draws on, Ed Stetzer and Daniel Im, *Planting Missional Churches* (Nashville: B&H Academic, 2016), p. 103.

It was at Antioch, however, that the followers of the Way were first described as 'Christians', a nickname applied from outside the church, giving them now a (potentially dangerous) recognisable identity separate from Judaism.

The church in Jerusalem continued to be mono-cultural, but in Antioch it quickly became multicultural. There was now a real danger that there would emerge two Christian denominations – Jewish and Gentile. Crucial to the development and unity of the early church was the recognition that now took place, under the guidance of the Holy Spirit – Jerusalem recognised Antioch. We can be certain that such change was painful on the ground. There is definitely an ominous sound about Acts 11:22, 'The report of this came to the ears of the church in Jerusalem'. Picture anxious, tense church meetings in the Jerusalem church – probably in Antioch as well. At which point, enter Barnabas, the Holy Spirit's man, the great encourager. He has the foresight to see that Paul himself is needed for this strategic work in Antioch: and so, the apostle Paul spends a whole year there, consolidating the work, giving weight to the 'grafting in' of the Gentiles (Rom. 11:17–24), encouraging the early church not only to tolerate its cultural diversity but to embrace it.

If you think that cultural diversity is a nice, but rather naïve, ideal for the Christian church today, think again and think Antioch. Think of the cost of such integration then, if you are daunted by its cost now. Think of a Jew from Jerusalem (Barnabas), another from Tarsus (Saul, a free Roman citizen), Simeon (or Niger, a black African), Lucius from Cyrene (the capital city of Libya), and Manaen, a longstanding friend of Herod the Tetrarch (Acts 13:1). In such a church the only qualifications for entry must surely be repentance and faith, not circumcision or adherence to food laws. You simply believed, then you really did belong: no first- and second-class Christians. Single-culture dominance was fading in Antioch. The church was beginning to reflect the ethnic and cultural demographic of the city, sending a powerful, prophetic message – a new community, a new family of God's people, all one in Christ, cultural enemies now become brothers and sisters. It is God's great plan for his church.

You must be adaptable

This kind of diversity, envisioned for the church in the New Testament, cannot exist and thrive without practising the biblical principle of accommodation. The Council of Jerusalem is the classic case. The Pauline texts about the conscience of a weaker brother, holy days, food laws and meat offered to idols are also relevant. Gospel foundations must never be removed (Ps. 11:3), but conditions in the Christian church must change as it develops over time.

The existence in most of the cities of the world today of scores of homogenous, mono-cultural local churches is testimony to how difficult cultural accommodation can be. Language is the most obvious obstacle to full cultural integration. In reality, however, there is a whole raft of other issues which would keep people of the same culture together, and from different cultures apart. Surely even these can, with strenuous effort, be overcome in order to aim for the true New Testament vision of the church of Jesus Christ confronting a culturally diverse world from its own experience and portrayal of inner cultural diversity.

Can this be done without compromise? The New Testament clearly shows that it can. In the New Testament there is never any adjustment to the 'faith that was once for all delivered to the saints' (Jude 3). There is always the understanding that in order to receive the gospel, people do not need cultural adaptations in the church, but the regenerating power of the Holy Spirit. As Paul writes, 'The natural person does not accept the things of the Spirit of God, for they are folly to him, and he is not able to understand them because they are spiritually discerned' (1 Cor. 2:14).

An ungodly culture, whether ancient, modern or postmodern, never actually asks for the gospel; it does not want it. The Jews may demand a sign, the Greeks may want wisdom, but our fixed purpose is to preach Christ crucified (1 Cor. 1:22). We do not give the world what it wants, but what it needs, depending entirely on the Holy Spirit to bring success to the message. We must never lose our nerve in proclaiming the good news of Jesus Christ whatever the culture. We must never apologise for the message or dilute it. In this we must practise absolute steadfastness.

Yet the church that first spread the gospel did become joyfully culturally diverse, and the apostles who preached it, though resolute about the things that are fixed, were also amazingly flexible about the things that are not.[4] They were determined that people from every cultural background should know that the gospel is indeed for them. A church whose own community life reflects and models this is a powerful witness. The gospel, never received and believed by all, is nonetheless *for* all.

When Paul preached to Jews, he did it in the synagogue on the seventh day of the week. He based his preaching on Old Testament texts. When he preached to Gentiles, he did it in any place, at any time. In Athens he began with creation and a declaration of the living God in contrast to their idols. He even quoted pagan poets. The content of what he said was determined by Scripture. His dependency was on the Holy Spirit, but his method was to engage with people where they were, and he did this without dumbing down.

New Testament believers were utterly convinced, as we are, that regeneration only takes place by the sovereign work of the Holy Spirit. They believed, as we do, that he is able to work through any channel of communication, such that engaging with the culture can be regarded only as a second order activity. Yet it is still the case that the gospel itself is in danger of being distorted, if it is presented as if it belonged to a single people group, or a monochrome culture. If our gospel proclamation only communicates with some people groups and not others, the gospel itself is in jeopardy.[5] However

---

4 See address by Stephen Clark: 'Fixed and Flexible', Banner of Truth Ministers' Conference 2003.

5 In Ephesians 3:6 the 'mystery' of the gospel is 'that the *Gentiles* (my emphasis) are fellow heirs, members of the same body, and

alien to a culture the message itself is, we need to find ways of communicating it in a manner that strikes chords with our hearers.

In the passage quoted above from 1 Corinthians 9:19–23, Paul is able to stand in other people's shoes. He puts himself where they are in order to bring the gospel to them. He gets inside their skin. The prophet Ezekiel did the same kind of thing with the exiles in Babylon – 'I sat where they sat' (Ezek. 3:15, NKJV). This is both vital for truly effective gospel work, and costly. It was in Paul's very bloodstream to be a Jew, a Hebrew of the Hebrews. He had impeccable Jewish ancestry and credentials. Now he had to adapt.

No one is saying that our native cultural heritage and identity is not ours. In another context Paul elucidates a principle that may have application outside its immediate context, 'each one should remain in the condition in which he was called'.[6] We are not trying to be what we are not. In a multicultural setting, the goal is not cultural assimilation but cultural accommodation. The simple, glorious reality is that the Christian gospel is not culture-bound. It is genuinely, radically cross-cultural. Every Christian is now a new person in Christ. Our new identity brings us to sit loosely to our old one. A new cultural reality trumps the original. Anywhere we go in the world, we can meet brothers and sisters in Christ

partakers of the promise in Christ Jesus through the gospel'.

6   See 1 Corinthians 7:20, where the teaching about marriage and singleness is that believers should be content to live in the social sphere to which God has assigned them, and live the life to which he has called them.

who are now closer to us than all our other natural associates. We are 'bound in the bundle of the living in the care of the LORD our God' (1 Sam. 25:29).

It follows that if I am in Christ and you are in Christ, then whoever you are, whatever your background, we both depend on the same Saviour and believe the same gospel – though we may understand it imperfectly. We are, therefore, in an unbreakable, indissoluble union with each other, however great the differences between us, whatever those differences may be. In human clubs and societies, people come together, often from a similar social background, with a common interest. Birds of a feather flock together. Golfers love to talk golf with other golfers; bird watchers share information with fellow twitchers. When this kind of behaviour is replicated in church, people come together because they share the same kind of social or religious background, or the same views on issues. The basis of our union, however, the spiritual reality which it expresses, is simply and ultimately not that we share the same opinions, but that we share the same Saviour. I do not say that theological and ecclesiastical points of difference between us are of no consequence, but that before and beyond all of them we share a fundamental spiritual unity. In church life we need to remind ourselves constantly of this spiritual reality. It is all too easy to drift off into the kind of mind-set that bases our unity on whether or not we agree about ways of doing things (styles of worship, for example). 'Unity' rooted in such things is biblically inauthentic and fragile. In the Christian church people come together fundamentally not because they share a cultural identity, or because they share the same denominational allegiance or viewpoint, or sense of religious heritage, but ultimately, solely, as drawn together by the same Holy Spirit and the same Lord Jesus Christ. It is 'unto him shall the gathering of the people be' (Gen. 49:10, AV).

To labour the point, it follows that in the diverse cultural setting in which a church is planted and it begins to grow, that church must recognise its fundamental unity in Christ while also affirming and accommodating to its cultural diversity. You would not expect to find in a local church a diversity that is not present in its neighbourhood. If there are no factory workers or students or Chinese or asylum seekers in the catchment of your church, you do not need to beat yourself up because there are none of them in your church. Yet you would hope, and pray and work to see the kind of diversity that is present in your community reflected in your local church. If a church is to be truly indigenous, it must be accessible to the people who live round it. If you truly believe in the Bible doctrine of election, you will look to see people of all kinds called into the kingdom (1 Cor. 1:26–31; 6:9–11).

This idea is usefully summed up in the Lausanne Covenant:

The gospel does not presuppose the superiority of any culture to another, but evaluates all cultures according to its own criteria of truth and righteousness, and insists on moral absolutes in every culture. Missions have, all too frequently, exported with the gospel an alien culture, and churches have sometimes been in bondage to culture rather than to Scripture. Christ's evangelists must humbly seek to empty themselves of all but their personal authenticity in order to become the servants of others, and churches must seek to transform and enrich culture, all for the glory of God.[7]

We are often so immersed in the church culture familiar to us that we are not even aware of it. If we define culture simply as 'the way we do things round here', when visitors walk into our churches, they are hit by it. It is wonderful if what hits them is a community of love.

Don Carson suggests that ideally the church is not composed of natural friends but rather natural enemies:

> What binds us together is not common education, common race, common income levels, common politics, common nationality, common accents, common jobs, or anything of the sort. Christians come together not because they form a natural collocation, but because they have been saved by Jesus Christ and owe him a common allegiance. In the light of this common allegiance, in the light of the fact that they have all been loved by Jesus himself, they commit to doing what he says – and he commands them to love one another. In this light they are a band of natural enemies who love one another for Jesus' sake.[8]

The believers in Corinth were dividing into factions. There was a party spirit. Their behaviour around the Lord's Supper left much to be desired (1 Cor. 1:10–17; 11:17–34). Things had developed in the church culture that needed to change. It was one of the great reasons the apostle found it necessary,

---

7   The Lausanne Covenant, section 10 'Evangelism and Culture' www. lausanne.org/content

8   Don Carson, *Love in Hard Places* (Wheaton: Crossway, 2002), p. 61.

under the inspiration of the Holy Spirit, to write to them. We continue to need the corrective power of the Word of God.

We are all equal

If the biblical principle of accommodation is vital to our understanding of the cultural fluidity of the church of Jesus, the principle of equality in Christ is even more so. Baseline, radical Bible teaching affirms unequivocally that Christians are 'all one in Christ Jesus' (Gal. 3:28). This unity goes beyond names, sects and parties to a genuine equality of personhood in Christ.[9] True, there are different, complementary roles for men and women. There is authority, order and appointed leadership in the church, home and workplace. Still the spiritual equality is real, not just ideal or projected into the future, but visibly demonstrated, incarnational in the church on earth. The church of Jesus is a surrogate family, a unique, cross-cultural community of the people of God – all ages, classes, ethnicities, levels of intelligence, status, wealth – all one and equal in Christ.

The New Testament is not a political document, though it has implications for politics. Its message is not *first* about social change. It may be asked, for example, why Paul does not protest about the slavery of his day. Yet his teaching about Christian masters and slaves is so radical that it must surely lead ultimately to Christian moves to abolish slavery (Eph. 6:5–9; 1 Tim. 6:1, 2; Phlm). The doctrine of equality in Christ is truly revolutionary.

---

9   See Charles Wesley's hymn, 'Lord from whom all blessings flow'.

The old paths

When I began my ministry, several well-meaning friends exhorted me to stick to 'the old paths'. I well knew what they meant and, as this story unfolds, you too will get a clearer picture. My problem was not in the concept of old paths, but in the suspicion that their old paths were not old enough! They did not go back far enough – only one hundred years or so; or at best four hundred. To rediscover the original old paths, we need to go back to the church at her beginning, in the first century AD, paths revealed and marked out in the New Testament. I am certainly not saying that the lessons learned and the practices formed from the Protestant Reformation onwards are irrelevant. We must do our church history and learn its lessons well. It is just that we cannot do that job well without also taking everything back to the original template. We must be reformed but always reforming under the Word of God.

Barnacles

The pick-and-mix religious diversity of our twenty-first-century culture, together with its openness to apparent spirituality, gives it a clear resonance with conditions when the glorious light of the gospel first shone into first-century darkness. The major difference, of course, is that the church then was new, young, vibrant and untrammelled by tradition. Twenty centuries of church history have complicated the picture.

The church of Jesus Christ can be likened to a great ship that has sailed grandly through two millennia. At the beginning, as depicted in the Acts of the Apostles, she sailed with spectacular glory. There have been times since then that have recaptured, almost, this former glory, but at other times the hulk of the glorious original seems to have become encrusted with barnacles.[10] There have been extra-biblical additions and traditions. She is in need of a deep clean. Are we called initially to a barnacle scraping ministry with the ship in dock but hopefully ready to sail? It may not be an easy or pleasant job. It may scrape the nerves of the scrapers as well as the bows of the ship, but it has to be done if, with a full international crew on board, she can be truly seaworthy again.

Living through the story of these pages, our work on a small scale in inner-city Coventry has seemed at times to be more about scraping off barnacles than being on board ship in full sail. With the particular subculture we inherited, we have been engaged in a bit more scraping than is perhaps common in a local church. Some will think we have been over-zealous, others not zealous enough. Readers must judge for themselves.

---

10 I am indebted to David Cook for this illustration, used in a sermon series on Acts.

Section One:
A case study

Chapter 1
Sent to Coventry

For forty-five years I have been involved in change in a local church in Coventry, for thirty-five of them as a pastor. The change has been significant and, taking the long view, even dramatic. It has been painful yet exhilarating. The journey goes on.

I do not believe I have been the driving catalyst for this change. More than some others around me, I have been reluctant to change, even resistant to it. This is not the story of a mover and shaker. The way I see it is that any change for the better has been God-prodded, gospel-driven.

The church that I have been privileged to serve, first as a member, then as a deacon, then as a pastor, had high walls of cultural distinctiveness and separation, especially when I first joined it in 1974. If it is true that every church has its own subculture, influenced by history, tradition or denominational allegiance, then Rehoboth Strict Baptist Chapel in Lower Ford Street, Coventry, had a clearly observable one.

I was brought up in Bedfordshire. My family had strong allegiance to a cluster of churches known as Gospel Standard

Strict and Particular Baptists.[11] Many of these people are deeply godly, and I learnt a great deal from them. I was converted[12] among them and felt strongly that I belonged. Some of the features of their church life include a deep reverence for God, a love of the Bible as the Word of God, belief in the doctrines of grace, and an emphasis on the vital necessity of the work of the Holy Spirit. The preaching, textual and experiential rather than expository, is, at its best, wonderfully Christ-centred. Joseph Hart's lines are much approved, 'True religion's more than notion, something must be known and felt.'[13]

However, this group of churches, in which I was so fully immersed in childhood and teenage years, was, and is, hyper-Calvinistic at least in its official doctrinal formulations. These go beyond mainstream Calvinism. Its denominational identity, separate even from other Strict Baptist and Grace Baptist Churches, is bound up with its articles of faith, especially its 'added articles', which attempt to circumscribe the way the gospel is to be presented.[14] This human construct results, perhaps inevitably, in a chill wind of fatalism with respect

---

11 Where 'strict' refers to the practice of communion, and 'particular' to the belief in particular redemption.

12 In this group of churches, the language of conversion is rarely used; the term 'called by grace' is preferred.

13 'Let us ask the important question, (Brethren be not too secure),
    What it is to be a Christian, how we may our hearts assure.
    Vain is all our best devotion, if on false foundations built;
    True religion's more than notion; something must be known and felt.'
    Joseph Hart, *Gadsby's Selection*, 237

14 See chapter 3: 'Statement of faith'.

both to evangelism and personal salvation. Preachers who try conscientiously to adhere to it are robbed of their commission to call upon people to repent and believe the gospel. Those who listen to them week by week tend to develop a deep introspection about personal election. It is rare to find among them Christians who are assured of their salvation. Yet there is a clear sense of identity as being 'a chapel person' or 'one of our people' even if you are not a church member. I grew up self-identifying as one of these 'Gospel Standard Strict Baptists', and I knew this made me different, not only from other people around me, but also from others who claimed to be Christians. The following features, among others, also continue to be characteristic of all Gospel Standard churches:

- Strict observance of Sunday as the Lord's Day, attending chapel twice on Sunday.

- A strong emphasis on reverence in worship – often resulting in an unfortunate affectation of voice in public prayer and preaching.

- The King James Version of the Bible is revered as the only acceptable English version, and as the benchmark of authority in Bible translation. All modern translations are viewed as a downgrade. The fact that the KJV is itself a translation of the original Hebrew and Greek manuscripts is not emphasised.

- A nineteenth-century selection of hymns known as *Gadsby's* has become the only approved hymnbook for public worship, so integral to the Gospel Standard subculture as to be often quoted almost on a par with the Bible. Because poetry is more memorable than prose, the tendency is for 'the word that drops in' – the convicting thought or the confirming promise – to be a hymn rather than a Bible verse.[15] Sermons, obituaries and testimonies often have more than a sprinkling of quotations from the hymnbook.

- The language used in prayer is Elizabethan English – 'thee' and 'thou'. There is also a phraseology instantly recognisable to the initiated, but which can be puzzling, even incomprehensible, to those who are 'outsiders'.

- There is a strong emphasis on Christian experience. Consecutive preaching of passages or books of the Bible is not generally approved. The expectation, and prayer, is that the preacher will be led to the right text for the occasion. Expository preaching does not fit easily into this mould, the fear being that such preaching becomes dry, academic, and is not Spirit-led.[16] Thus, preachers should meditate and pray over the Word but not prepare their sermons to the extent that they take notes into the pulpit. The culture is of extemporary prayer and preaching, with an immediate sense of being guided by the Holy Spirit. On

---

15 The need for a word to be applied personally to the soul by the Holy Spirit is emphasised. That word of course is very often from the Bible but it seems to carry equal weight when it is from a hymn.

16 One pastor ran into trouble with his church when he began to preach consecutively through the Acts of the Apostles: see Bernard J. Honeysett, *The Sound of His Name* (Edinburgh: Banner of Truth, 1995).

occasions a preacher might be still wrestling for 'a text' in the hymn before the sermon! It is not surprising if such lack of preparation soon becomes uncomfortably evident to the congregation. It has to be said, however, that the more able ministers of this connection do carefully prepare their sermons with prayer and study, and there is structure and order, as well as unction, in their preaching.

- Communion is restricted to church members or members of churches of the same faith and order (i.e. only other Gospel Standard Churches). The Lord's Supper is held once a month as a separate service. The communicants are usually a relatively small proportion of the whole congregation.

- Baptism is by total immersion upon profession of repentance towards God and faith in the Lord Jesus Christ. Because of the emphasis on experience, many hold back from this step, feeling that they do not have the requisite experience. Many of my own generation who have remained in these churches have yet to make a public profession of faith and to be baptised.

- A dress code for worship. Women and girls are expected to have their heads covered. Strangely, over the years, this wearing of hats has become, among some, quite showy, almost a fashion statement. At the same time women's trousers and make up are frowned on, not only for chapel but for everyday life. Men and boys are usually expected to wear jackets and ties for worship.

- A clearly understood sense of what constitutes 'worldliness' – going to the cinema or theatre, or owning a television for example. Yet, in the 1950s and '60s, when I was growing up, smoking and the moderate use of alcohol did not carry the same taboo. It was not unusual even to find a Gospel Standard minister who smoked.

- Missionary interest and involvement is limited. There is strong support for the Bible Society which translates and distributes the Scriptures worldwide but confines itself to the KJV for all English publications. Other missionary enterprises can be approved (usually because of the involvement of people from Gospel Standard Churches) but always with caution, lest it brings unhelpful contact with churches of a different 'faith and order'.

- There is a strong sense of belonging to a denomination, and of separation between this and other denominations. There is an approved list of Gospel Standard Churches and recognised Gospel Standard ministers. Its charitable and denominational life is organised by a committee, which in effect carries significant authority within the denomination.

Though there may be arguments in favour of any, or all, of these distinctive features, taken together they undoubtedly constitute a recognisable and identifiable subculture. There is a real sense in which one needs to be initiated in order to belong, and the easiest way to belong is to be born into a

Gospel Standard family. The term 'outsiders' is used in a quite unselfconscious way for people who may come to chapel who, it is realised, do not come from the same background.

These strong influences on my life meant that when I began a teachers' training course in Coventry in 1969, it was completely natural, and expected, for me to seek out Rehoboth in Lower Ford Street, which had been a strong Gospel Standard Church.

In this particular church, however, there had been some significant recent developments. It had appointed a pastor who could not himself adhere to the 'added' articles of faith, and who made this clear at the commencement of his ministry in Coventry. He was not on the approved list of ministers. His ministry was more expository in style than was the norm, and there were some people in the church – then in a minority – who were not fully signed up to the Gospel Standard position.

Most of the classic identifying features of a Gospel Standard Strict Baptist church were, nonetheless, still in place. The church was still on the list of Gospel Standard churches and still only had fellowship with other Strict Baptist churches. It took a separatist stance from other reformed and evangelical churches in Coventry and district, and even from Grace Baptist churches locally and nationally. Its communion table was closed to Christians from a wider circle of churches.

This is the church in which I was baptised and became a member in 1974. Having met my wife, Hazel, at the chapel, we were married there in 1975. In many ways we were blessed and happy. I was teaching. We started a family. We were fed and helped by the ministry of our pastor.

Then the church began to go through a painful time of upheaval. There were those who wanted to safeguard the identity of the church as Gospel Standard Strict Baptist, and who were therefore resistant even to minor changes or reformation. Some in the church had relatives and friends who were members of non-Gospel Standard churches, who, when they visited Rehoboth, found that the rule on communion caused a sad separation at the Lord's Table. The same rule applied when Rehoboth members visited their churches. Was this right? The issue would not go away. The pastor also wanted to introduce the singing of metrical Psalms in addition to the use of *Gadsby's* hymns, but any proposal of change was strenuously resisted by a small, vocal group. Church meetings became tense and difficult and feelings ran high.

The straw that finally broke the camel's back was a strange issue. Many evangelicals today will find it almost incomprehensible. It is important to our subject because it indicates vividly how churches can develop their own subculture, circumscribing themselves, and others, with extra-biblical rules and requirements.

In January 1976, an editorial in the denominational magazine expressed the view that it would be 'worldly' and inconsistent for members of Gospel Standard churches to possess a television in their homes. Going beyond a straightforward warning of the dangers of TV, a directive was issued which was calculated to bind people's consciences: 'May pastors and deacons be given grace to exercise discipline in this solemn matter in the case of church members.'[17]

Given the influence of the magazine, the repercussions of this statement were bound to be felt in many churches. Mere possession of a TV, it was now decreed, should be a matter of church order and discipline. There were those in the church at Rehoboth – including the two deacons, but not the pastor – who wanted to enforce this rule. Someone applied to be baptised and join the church who owned a TV, but was not prepared to get rid of it in order to become a church member. They felt that this was a matter of Christian liberty and conscience (after all televisions do have an on/off switch!). This issue, catapulted into the church from outside, caused great confusion and strife within. The upshot was that both longstanding deacons resigned because in their view the church was not taking a clear enough line. Two young men in our late-twenties, Peter Cordle and I, found ourselves appointed in their place. The only elder at that time was the pastor, the model of a church led by pastor and deacons having been followed by the church from its inception.[18]

No doubt those who wanted to enforce this rule were motivated, with the best construction on it, by a fear of worldliness and a passion for purity of testimony in the church of Jesus Christ. Yet, however good and godly the instincts, to insist on time-bound extra-biblical rules, and to compromise

---

17 'New Year address', *The Gospel Standard*, January 1976, p. 6.

18 Though taking the whole history of the church there have been as many years without a pastor as with one, thereby enhancing the responsibilities of the deacons in office in those pastor-less periods.

genuine Christian freedom of conscience, will inevitably lead to confusion and double standards. The debate that took place in our church in the 1970s is now, in the light of the whole digital revolution, strangely obsolete. Possession of a TV, however used, was then taken as itself a mark of worldliness. Now the very same people who probably still would not on principle have a TV in their homes, have access through many other screens and devices to almost all the same material, and more. The Internet revolution means that everyone now needs the discipline of the on/off switch.

More seriously, it must be apparent that if a church has a rule that you cannot become a member if you own a TV, this can then become a serious disincentive to evangelism. Can you really expect to bring the message of salvation to the people in your community without unnecessary obstacles, if one of your early duties is to counsel them to get rid of their TV as a sign of their repentance and receiving the message of the gospel?

As a result of these tensions in the church, it was perhaps inevitable that some kind of split would occur. A number of people, both in membership and in the wider congregation, who adhered to the denominational line, moved to a Gospel Standard Church in a neighbouring town. Such division is always very sad. Rehoboth was now left somewhat reduced in numbers, but also beginning to feel a little more free to conduct its life and ministry according to biblical, rather than denominational, convictions.

It was during this time that God began to place on me an inescapable sense of calling to preach the gospel. I was by now head of Religious Studies in an independent grammar school. Whilst I enjoyed teaching, and had considerable freedom in that school in how I taught, there always had to be an element of 'sitting on the fence'. God was now placing on me a new burden. People's greatest need is for the gospel, and for a time in my life it seemed that wherever I went, whatever I read, whatever preaching I heard, I was being challenged by this need. My personal Bible reading sometimes seemed to be opening up in a way that was for others as well as for me.

Eventually, and very hesitantly, I shared this growing sense of call first with my grandfather, still, in his early-eighties, a pastor in Bedfordshire, then with my own pastor. It transpired that this did not come as a complete surprise to either man, and in other ways God had been paving the way. The result was that 'a call to preach' was recognised within the church at Rehoboth. In 1982 I began an itinerant preaching ministry, almost entirely in Gospel Standard churches, where my family connections meant that I was known and, at least to begin with, considered 'acceptable'. I was teaching in the week and preaching every Sunday in chapels across a wide geographical area. By this time, our family had grown to include three children.

This itinerant ministry in Gospel Standard churches was in many ways, even for me, an eye-opener. Many of them were in a low state both numerically and spiritually, meeting the needs of a dwindling constituency. There was little vision and little, if any, concern about reaching their communities with the gospel. People attended because they were 'chapel'. They and their families had always done so. They seemed oblivious to the barriers of language, dress and general presupposition for the uninitiated. The subculture I was experiencing on a Sunday, though of course familiar to me from childhood, was light years away from one in which I could communicate the gospel message to the children and colleagues at school. Could I ever realistically invite any of them to hear me preach in that context? There were barriers that were nothing to do with the gospel itself. Were these barriers biblical?

In 1983 the pastor at Rehoboth accepted a call to a similar church in East Sussex, and consequently I began to do more ministry at home. Around this time, I was offered a promotion to the role of head of Lower School. A strong career move, it was a position that held a lot of attraction. By then, however, I knew that God was calling me eventually into full-time ministry. After a memorable weekend of inward struggle, I explained to the head teacher the reason why I felt I must let this opportunity pass me by.

During 1984 I preached at our home church in Coventry regularly, and it became clear that there was a growing sense that this was with a view to becoming the next pastor. It became my urgent prayer that God would guide me into his will for me and for the church at Rehoboth. The situation was complicated by the fact that around that time I received several enquiries from other churches about becoming their pastor. Then the call came from my fellow-members at Rehoboth – a warm and unanimous invitation to be their pastor. Two particular passages from the Bible settled the matter for me. The first:

'So as much as in me is, I am ready to preach the gospel to you that are at Rome also' (Rom. 1:15, AV).[19] This expressed how I felt about preaching the gospel, and it encouraged me in a particular focus. For me it was not Rome, but Coventry. The second passage was:

> The elders which are among you I exhort, who am also an elder, and a witness of the sufferings of Christ, and also a partaker of the glory that shall be revealed: Feed the flock of God which is among you, taking the oversight thereof, not by constraint but willingly; not for filthy lucre, but of a ready mind; Neither as being lords over God's heritage, but being ensamples [examples] to the flock. And when the chief Shepherd shall appear, ye shall receive a crown of glory that fadeth not away. (1 Pet. 5.1-4, AV)

An interesting connection between these two texts is the concept of readiness, or eagerness, but the phrase that particularly stood out for me was 'the flock of God which is among you'. The people at Rehoboth were already in my heart. I was already labouring among them.

I accepted the call, and so began my pastoral ministry at Rehoboth in 1985. There were at that time about fifteen active church members and an average Sunday morning congregation of almost forty, including children.

It was an exclusively white, mostly middle-class congregation of people who drove to 'chapel' because of the type of church it was. It is interesting to reflect on the fact that in the original trust deed of the 'Rehoboth Particular Baptist

19 I am quoting from the AV as that was the version I used then.

Chapel' building, dated 31 October 1857, the occupations of the original trustees are listed as baker, watchmaker, ribbon manufacturer, cordwainer, gardener, tollgate keeper and several weavers. By 1985, taking people's occupations, the congregation had become somewhat upwardly mobile.

When I began my ministry at Rehoboth, many of the distinctive features of the Gospel Standard Strict Baptist church subculture were still firmly in place.[20] The Bible version used in church and Sunday school was the KJV. The only hymnbook in use was *Gadsby's*, with very occasional use of metrical psalms. The singing, accompanied by a pedal harmonium, was very slow. The church leadership structure was a pastor and deacons, there being by that time three deacons. The term 'elder' was not in the church's normal vocabulary. The prayer meetings were conducted by calling only on men to pray – often to announce a hymn of their choice first, then to pray. It was not unusual for a man to pray for ten to fifteen minutes. The women, who were all expected to have their heads covered for worship, did not pray audibly. The communion, open only to church members and visiting baptised believers of the same faith and order of churches, was held as a separate service once a month, after the evening service.

The chapel building was regarded somewhat as a sanctuary, a kind of sacred space. This impacted how children and people generally were expected to behave 'in the house of God'. In 1985 the building was largely as it had been in 1857. In the 1970s

---

20 See pp. 45-48.

there had been a single storey redevelopment at the rear of the building, including a meeting room, minister's vestry, small kitchen and toilets. The chapel itself was filled with pews, and most people sat well back because the pulpit was in an elevated position. The deacon announced ('gave out') the hymns from a desk below the pulpit. Casual dress for public worship was frowned upon; the wearing of trousers and make up by women not approved.

At the same time, it should be noted that the ministry of my predecessor had prepared the way for some change to be envisaged, and gradually to take place. As already observed, his ministry was more exegetical and evangelistic than was the norm in Gospel Standard Churches. This had attracted people, including some students, from a non-Gospel Standard background. Some latitude had been given in matters of dress and mode of expression in prayer, for example. A concern for outreach was expressed and prayed about. For many years there had been an afternoon Sunday School for neighbourhood children as well as for chapel families.

None of the features that characterised our church life then were, in and of themselves, insuperable barriers to people hearing and receiving the gospel. The Holy Spirit is well able to work above and beyond and through all of them. But it is still true to say that when I began my ministry, the church had a defined subculture which, for anyone who was alien to it, created significant obstacles to hearing and receiving the message of salvation, as some of us were increasingly coming to realise. That was serious.

Chapter 2
Where there is no vision

Change came slowly and painfully. Immersed as I was from childhood in the Strict Baptist way of doing things, I myself was part of the need to change, if the gospel through me, and the people with me, was to reach a wider, more diverse group of people. My exposure at university to liberal theology, which I had vigorously but rather ineptly opposed, had, by God's grace, confirmed me more and more in the grand certainties of orthodox biblical Christianity. Experiencing contact with genuine evangelical Christians from other denominations and traditions had, I hope, fostered a little more humility. 'We are the people and the truth will die with us' no longer seemed a tenable mantra.

There was now a growing burden to bring to all kinds of people the one message they most need – the gospel without cultural baggage and distraction, without hindrance. Right from the beginning of my ministry at Rehoboth, and even before I had officially begun as pastor, I found myself trying to discharge this sense of need for greater impact for the gospel. I was preaching, first of all, to myself.

However, it would be a mistake and a false impression to imply that all this was happening just to me, or that I was carrying the burden alone. Since the beginning of the 'troubles' in the church, there were a number of us who were being stirred up to seek God's blessing in a new way. One of the features of the whole of my pastoral ministry is that I have been greatly helped and supported by godly, gifted men and women of vision and of great spiritual calibre and encouragement. These people do not need to be named; they know who they are. Some are now with the Lord. Without them, under God, none of it would have happened. Their role will, I hope, become increasingly apparent as the story unfolds.

The neighbourhood of Rehoboth Chapel has changed significantly since Victorian times. At one time it was a fairly genteel residential neighbourhood. Then, being on the edge of the city centre, light industry began to take over. Factories sprang up, and the mostly terraced housing served their workers. The munitions factories were famously targeted in the Blitz on Coventry in November 1940, bringing the danger and damage very close to the chapel. The nearby Cathedral took a big hit, but amazingly only a few tiles were dislodged from the roof of Rehoboth Chapel. By the 1960s and '70s, the district of Hillfields, as the area is now known, had gone into sharp decline. High rise blocks of flats were built. It became a social priority area. Drug pushers and users, moneylenders and prostitutes were part of the scene. In more recent years there has been an element of revitalisation, boosted especially by the burgeoning growth of Coventry University and its need for student accommodation. Ever-growing numbers of students have found a home in Hillfields, many of them in purpose-built accommodation blocks, many others in student lets. Hillfields today has a very cosmopolitan population. In its central square there are businesses run by Poles, Iraqis, Afghans and other Asians, to name only a few. Refugees and asylum seekers are here from all over the world; people of all religions and none. Slowly, very slowly, the burden began to grow within Rehoboth Chapel, Lower Ford Street, to try to bring the gospel to these very people.

In the early years of my ministry at Rehoboth I preached a couple of sermons which were watershed moments both for me, and, I think, for the church. The first of these was a sermon on Proverbs 29:18 preached in my first year of ministry in November 1982, well before I was appointed pastor. In the KJV the text reads 'Where there is no vision the people perish: but he that keepeth the law, happy is he' (AV). The sermon noted the importance of 'vision' in every aspect of life, but especially traced the highs and lows of prophetic revelation in biblical history. It identified the vision, or open revelation, ultimately as the gospel itself, and referred to the new era of gospel preaching marked by Peter on the Day of Pentecost and Paul at Athens, for example. Acts 17:30 was quoted: 'the time of this ignorance God winked at, but now commandeth all men everywhere to repent' (AV). The force of that, contra the Gospel Standard 'added articles' of faith, was felt.

The sermon made an attempt to identify what the vision looks and feels like – an awareness of the awesome majesty of

God, a conviction of sin, a realisation of the need for salvation. Let me give you a flavour of this novice sermon with an excerpt from near its conclusion:

> Are we people of vision? What do we want as we think about the future? Do we want things to stay as they always have done? Do we want to put the clock back and have things as they were thirty, forty, fifty years ago? Or do we have a vision for more of the sense of the presence of God as we meet together? Do we want to know as we meet together that God is of a surety with us? Do we have a vision of the church of Jesus Christ in which its members are drawn closer together in a bond of spiritual union and fellowship, in which people take knowledge of us that we have been with Jesus? Do we have a vision of a church that is no longer like an exclusive organisation in which people no longer strive for status or power? In which men and women and boys and girls are drawn from all walks of society, from all types and racial backgrounds, in which the one thing which draws them together is the everlasting gospel of Jesus Christ?

Such preaching in that context, though elementary and unexceptional, was set to bring change.

The second watershed sermon was preached in November 1985 – the first year of my pastorate. The text was Isaiah 54:1–3:

> Sing, O barren, thou that didst not bear; break forth into singing, and cry aloud, thou that didst not travail with child: for more are the children of the desolate than the children of the married wife, saith the LORD.

Enlarge the place of thy tent, and let them stretch forth the curtains of thine habitations: spare not, lengthen thy cords and strengthen thy stakes; For thou shalt break forth on the right hand and on the left; and thy seed shall inherit the Gentiles, and make the desolate cities to be inhabited (AV).

The sermon noted that the blessings of Isaiah 54 flow out of the powerful prophecies of Isaiah 53 – the suffering and death of the Messiah and its wonderful fruits. The barren woman addressed by the Lord through the prophet is, first, Israel in captivity, but ultimately the church of Jesus Christ. The great promises of the chapter are promises of good things to come. The church will be established. She will grow. She will be fruitful. God himself will be her protector. These promises were especially fulfilled on the Day of Pentecost and have been, in different measures, ever since.

The barren woman is to be active in two areas – the lengthening of cords, the strengthening of stakes. She is now expectant, so she is stitching new canvas. She is extending her tent. She is getting the nursery ready. It is a vivid picture of change, the upheaval that comes with new arrivals.

Picture a young couple who have been struggling with infertility. Suddenly the woman is pregnant. There is great excitement, expectation, activity. They dedicate a bedroom for the nursery. They redecorate it, get it all ready. Perhaps they go over the top with the colour scheme. Everyone knows that when the baby arrives things will never be the same again. The change will be a lot more far-reaching than a few outward adjustments. Nonetheless, it is eagerly anticipated. It is *welcome* change. The barren woman *sings*. We all know that it will not come without cost and considerable upheaval.

The two kinds of activity – lengthening of cords, strengthening of stakes – point to things that need to be done commensurately in preparation for growth. The lengthening of the cords is about making room. It is about vision, evangelism, outreach. It is about faith and expectation. In his hymn 'Jesus where'er thy people meet', William Cowper challenges our restricted vision of sacred space. 'Every place', he says, where Jesus is sought and found 'is hallowed ground'. The original hymn has a verse not usually included in hymnbooks today:

> *Behold at thy commanding Word*
> *We stretch the curtains and the cord:*
> *Come thou and fill this wider space*
> *And bless us with a large increase!*

In those days, our building was plenty big enough to take more people, but our prayer was that the Lord would bless us with many more spiritual children as envisaged by the prophet Malachi:

> 'Try me now in this,' says the LORD of hosts. 'If I will not open for you the windows of heaven and pour out for you such blessing that there will not be room enough to receive it' (Mal. 3:10, NKJV).

It was our longing then and still is today.

The other activity – strengthening the stakes – is of commensurate importance to stretching the fabric. It is about securing and stabilising the tent. The 1985 sermon identified five specific 'stakes':

1. The absolute authority of the Word of God in all matters of church life and practice.

2. The great doctrines of grace: the doctrine of the gospel itself.

3. The free preaching and teaching of this gospel.

4. The need for believers to be 'rooted and grounded in love' (Eph. 3:17) – love for God, love for one another.

5. The need for believers to obey the Word of God, to practise the gospel as in Colossians 2:7 – 'Rooted and built up in him, and stablished in the faith, as ye have been taught, abounding therein with thanksgiving' (AV).

The list is not exhaustive, but the stakes need to be driven down deeper *at the same time* as the guy-ropes are lengthened. It is not a case of the one or the other. Imagine a very small tent with massive stakes. Everything is safe and cosy in there, but there is no vision or preparation for growth, no lengthening of cords. Some churches tragically fit the profile. Picture on the other hand a vast tent, like a marquee, but with inadequate support, feeble tent pegs. The first major gust of wind will bring it down. Some churches and church movements are all outreach, little depth.

Isaiah 54 was, of course, the great catalyst for the modern missionary movement. Here is a geography teacher who, as he points out the various countries of the world to the children in his class, sheds tears. He is crying because of all the people who have never heard of Jesus. He is teaching in a village school in Northamptonshire. A few years later, in 1792, the same man is preaching in Nottingham, at an association meeting of Particular Baptist churches. His name is William Carey. He preaches from Isaiah 54. His sermon will produce the motto – 'Expect great things from God, attempt great things for God' – divine dependence, human enterprise. It was in this context that Carey suffered the famous 'put down' in a ministers' meeting of the same association. As he was pleading for commitment and action, and the formation of 'A Society for Propagating the Gospel Among the Heathen', an older minister interrupted him in full flow, 'Young man, sit down! ... When God is pleased to convert the heathen, he will do it without consulting you or me.' This spirit is not dead. Such a sentiment, sadly, has a familiar ring to me from my hyper-Calvinist roots.

I mention these two sermons because I wish to emphasise that gospel-driven change in our church in Coventry came about as a result of preaching the Word of God. This is not to claim that all the change that has taken place has been right, or managed well, but that the vision we have tried to keep in the forefront of our thinking and praying is the desire to be obedient to God's Word. In our case there was a lot of work to be done to get the nursery ready, so that our church could become a place where new spiritual children could be born and nurtured.

It is surely instinctive and biblical for any church to cry out to God for revival. However, it is worth asking what kind of growth we are envisaging. Our vision may be constrained by unbiblical parameters. For some, the extent of the vision is evangelism by reproduction. They hope that existing Christians will have big families, and these will populate the church. For others, their vision of growth is by relocation. They hope that likeminded Christians will move in from other areas, or that people dissatisfied with other local churches may relocate to 'our' church. As has often been observed, such a clannish approach to Christianity is not real growth. It raises real questions about motive. Are we only really interested in the survival of our church, the shoring up of its future, the maintenance of an institution that we know and love? Each local church should rather be praying for the kind of growth that comes from the people being reached who live in its neighbourhood, and God's elect people being saved. Local churches are not to be little islands of subculture. Rather, they are to be a lighthouse, even the rescue boat itself, to reach out to those who are lost and despairing in a troubled sea.

If and when our prayers are answered, what then? I think we can all see that change is inevitable. Life means change.

Chapter 3
The hare or the tortoise?

In the first decade of my ministry, gospel-driven change, though significant over that period of time, took a measured, some would say tortoise-like, pace. Partly this was due to my own inherent conservatism and reluctance to change. Partly it was because there were still those in the church and congregation who were strongly resistant to almost any change. It was also because through most of that time we were still under the watchful and critical eye of the denominational body to which, historically, we had belonged. In addition, there was a familial reality: my own father was a member of the Gospel Standard committee and passionately committed to preserving the distinctive, separatist stance of the denomination.

I would like to think that the slow pace of change was also partly because we were sensitive to God's timing. Looking back on it, I can see that I was perhaps in a strong position to lead this particular congregation through the changes that we began to initiate, coming from the background I did. At least I was able to understand and empathise with those who were resistant to change, at the same time enjoying a measure of their confidence. If the pace of change had been fast and furious in those early days, we would scarcely have carried the people with us. Being born into the culture, sharing its hang-ups, was in a way a strength – no doubt in other ways a weakness. Issues of gospel-driven change came for me with a lot of emotional and relationship baggage. God makes no mistakes, however, and looking back I can see his overruling goodness and kindness.

One of the principles we have learnt – of which more can be said later – is that there is not only a right thing to do, but a right time to do it. Again, I do not say that we always got the timing right. However, timing is very important to managing change in the local church, as I believe our story illustrates. At the same time, it is important not to lose the edge of gospel urgency. With hindsight some of the issues that were causing observable impediments in bringing the gospel to unchurched people could have been handled more decisively and courageously.

Reaching out

The parable of the mustard seed is nonetheless encouraging to small beginnings. In our meetings of pastor and deacons, and in members' meetings, we began to explore what our vision might look like in the local community. We dared to use a word like 'strategy'. We started to find out more about what was going on in Hillfields. We began to produce our own evangelistic leaflets and to distribute them locally. In 1986, two members were formally commissioned by the church to do visitation work in the neighbourhood of the chapel, and so a door-to-door ministry began which still goes on today. Such a thing had never been done in the church before.

Through a contact from someone in our congregation, a Bible study began in a hostel in another part of the city. A small group began to conduct services in a local warden-controlled home for the elderly. The idea germinated that we could open up our church premises as a drop-in centre. This was eventually launched in 1992 and ran for over twenty years. Using the rear meeting room and kitchen, 'Daybreak' provided a welcome, friendship and free refreshments. It developed a regular clientele, mostly men on the fringes of society, some just lonely, others with an addiction of some kind. There were many opportunities for discussion and to bring the gospel to these dear people. There were some encouraging stories,[21] and a lot of cases where we seemed to see no change in people's lives at all.

Later on, Daybreak developed an extra arm through 'Chat Shack', a gazebo type arrangement that took Christian literature and free refreshments into the central square in Hillfields with the aim of opening up conversations about the gospel. It was only later that we discovered that khat is a drug yielding plant, used extensively in north-east Africa, and that some people's initial interest in our stall was motivated by something completely different! We were certainly beginning to experience the cultural diversity of our neighbourhood.

---

21 See chapter 6: 'Slices of Life'.

Statement of faith

When I began as pastor in 1985, the church was in a somewhat anomalous situation with regard to its statement of faith. Its trust document of 1857 states that the chapel building is:

> ... to be used, occupied and enjoyed as a place of Religious Worship by the Society or Congregation of Protestant Dissenters called Particular or Calvinistic Baptists proposing to assemble thereat maintaining the Doctrines of the one living and true God:
>
> - three equal persons in the God-head
> - eternal and personal Election
> - original sin
> - particular redemption
> - free justification by the imputed righteousness of Christ
> - Regeneration, Conversion and sanctification by the Spirit and Grace of God
> - the precepts of the Gospel a rule of life and conduct to all believers
> - the final perseverance of the Saints, the resurrection of the Body to eternal Life
> - the future Judgment
> - the eternal happiness of the righteous
> - and everlasting misery of such as die impenitent
> - and practising Baptism by immersion to such only as are of years of understanding upon their own confession of repentance towards God and faith in and obedience to our

Lord Jesus Christ[22]

These twelve one-liners are still incorporated in our members' handbook and have proved to be a providential source of continuity in the confessional life of the church.

It appears that at some point in the early or mid-twentieth century the Gospel Standard articles of faith, including the 'added articles', were adopted and incoming members required to signify their agreement with them. A search of the church minute books, however, fails to yield reference to any formal adoption. This became especially relevant at the point of our ejection from the Gospel Standard list of churches in 1992. We were then able to refer to our trust document as our defining constitution rather than to the Gospel Standard articles.

In 1985, however, it was still the church practice to ask new members to agree to these articles 'so far as they understood them'. The caveat existed especially to help people who had difficulty with the added articles. After all, even the pastor of the last eighteen years had expressed his difficulty and lack of support for those particular articles as phrased.[23]

Article 26 of the Gospel Standard articles reads as follows:

---

22 Capitals, but not bullet points, as per deed.

23 Over the years, various attempts have been made to explain these articles and reconcile them to Scripture – notably one by J.K. Popham, a well-known Gospel Standard minister and pastor of Galeed Chapel, Brighton 1882–1936. In my early years of ministry, I was asked whether I could agree to Popham's statement in order for my name to appear in advertised services on the wrapper of the *Gospel Standard Magazine*. As the statement does amount to a kind of modification of the added articles, at the time I agreed.

We deny duty faith and duty repentance – these terms signifying that it is every man's duty to spiritually and savingly repent and believe. We deny also that there is any capability in man by nature to any spiritual good whatever. So that we reject the doctrine that men in a state of nature should be exhorted to believe in or turn to God.

The key statements of the added articles are then:

Article 32:

We believe that it would be unsafe, from the brief records we have of the way in which the apostles, under the immediate direction of the Lord, addressed their hearers in certain special cases and circumstances, to derive absolute and universal rules for ministerial addresses in the present day under widely different circumstances ...

Article 33:

Therefore, that for ministers in the present day to address unconverted persons, or indiscriminately all in a mixed congregation, calling upon them to savingly repent, believe and receive Christ, or perform any other acts dependent upon the new creative power of the Holy Ghost, is on the one hand, to imply creature power, and, on the other, to deny the doctrine of special redemption.

Article 34:

We believe that any such expressions as convey to the hearers the belief that they possess a certain power to flee to the Saviour, to close in with Christ, to receive Christ, while in an unregenerate state, so that unless they do thus close with Christ etc, they shall perish, are untrue, and must, therefore, be rejected ...

These articles are by definition 'added' to the historic statements of the reformed faith. For a group of churches so committed to old paths, it is perhaps surprising that such confidence and significance is invested in doctrinal formulations that are relatively recent.[24] The reality is that they have come to delineate a separate and distinct position that is now jealously guarded.

The attempt to frame articles of faith that define the way the gospel is to be presented by the minister and received by the hearer is fundamentally misconceived, especially when it applies a logic that goes beyond the Word of God. In the Bible, the great realities of divine sovereignty and human accountability are held in perfect tension and counter-balance. Though these articles are motivated and informed by the biblical teaching that salvation is by grace alone, and that we are not able to contribute anything whatever towards our salvation, conclusions are then deduced that cannot be supported by Scripture, and terms used that are alien to it. The reference to the New Testament passages on apostolic preaching as 'brief records' betrays a worrying approach to biblical exegesis – and a surprising one among those who claim a high view of Scripture. The outcome is a kind of straitjacket

---

24 The Gospel Standard articles of faith went through several editions, leading to a list of 31 articles being published in 1872, to which the four more controversial articles were added in 1878.

for preachers of the gospel, restricting their freedom of expression in calling on people freely to receive and believe the good news, always in dependence on the vital, sovereign work of the Holy Spirit.[25]

That the church in Lower Ford Street was, in 1985, still using a statement of faith which held such difficulty for us is an indicator of how slow we had been so far to initiate gospel-driven change. From the beginning of my pastorate, however, we recognised the need for a doctrinal statement which was faithful to the Word of God, and which met the needs of incoming members for accuracy and comprehension. We began work on a short, yet biblically comprehensive, statement of faith that could be understood by all new applicants for membership. This eventually became the key section in a members' handbook that included a brief history of the church, its original trust document statement of faith, a section on the responsibilities of church members entitled 'The Local Church and Church Life', and a statement of church rules. Later, with the recognition of the office of elder, the church also adopted the fuller 1689 Baptist Confession of Faith, requiring all its elders and deacons to signify their agreement to it, but not requiring other members formally to do so. All this took place over years rather than months.

One of the early decisions, however, made in 1986, was to remove the word 'Strict' from our outside noticeboard. The term refers, of course, to strict communion: that is,

---

25 For a fuller treatment of this subject see, Geoff Haddow, A *Parable of a Garden* (Independently Published, 2019).

communion restricted to baptised believers of the same faith and order. Many in the church felt, however, that the only thing that 'strict' communicates to passers-by or the general public is some kind of austerity or exclusiveness. This relatively minor change did not happen without opposition. Since then, the church's position on communion has evolved to a degree, as we shall see.

Bible version

In 1985 the church Bible was the Authorised (or King James) Version, used in all the ministries, including children's work. Many pastors and churches will testify that it is not an easy or straightforward matter to change the Bible version used in a church, especially if that church has come from an 'AV only' mind-set. Firstly, of course, one needs to be persuaded it is the right thing to do. Personally, I needed quite a bit of persuasion and it took time. After all, there was a rationale – an inherited confidence in the received text on which it is based and a belief that for centuries God had owned and blessed the AV.

Yet, as time went on, we found that we could not be so dismissive of other translations, after seeing their integrity and the manuscript evidence behind them. The ultimate authority must always be the original manuscripts in Hebrew and Greek, and translation into the receptor language must be as accurate and accessible as possible. With the passage of time and changes in language and culture, doubts began to develop as to whether the AV was now achieving this.

One thing that had changed at Rehoboth before my time,

in the 1970s, was the recognition that most people now find it more natural to address God in prayer as 'you' and 'your' rather than 'thee' and 'thou'. Until then, to use the more everyday mode of address had been considered too familiar, even irreverent. Even when I began my ministry there was still a certain stigma associated with it. All the churches I then preached in were AV churches, and expected their ministers to address God as 'thee' or 'thou' – which requires a certain adaptation, even convolution, of the associated language. At Rehoboth, however, there was now latitude on this.

The Bible itself does not reflect a two-tier approach to language – a kind of religious or theological utterance as well as an everyday usage. Elizabethan English was definitely the vernacular when the KJV was first produced. As a teacher of Religious Studies, I knew I would have great difficulty in insisting on using the KJV in school, although I did have a colleague in the English department, with no interest in Christian things, who was nonetheless in favour of me doing so in order that his pupils would be better equipped to study Shakespeare!

We clung on to the AV for many years at Rehoboth but with a growing sense of uneasiness and mismatch. There were factors that were too persistent to go away. One was the barrier we found as teachers using the AV to speak to children in church and Sunday school, especially children from the neighbourhood. This perceived difficulty became even more acute when we found ourselves teaching the Bible to people for whom English was a second language. I was to have the privilege, for example, of studying the Bible with Iranian asylum seekers, freshly into this country, whose knowledge of English was, at that point, almost non-existent. I became their main teacher of English and did it through the Bible – but how could I have done so if I had insisted on teaching them through language forms they would never encounter in their daily lives? Is it really part of our duty in bringing such people the truth of God's Word to explain such phrases as 'evil concupiscence', 'superfluity of naughtiness' and 'I wot not', quite apart from the fact that words like 'conversation' now mean something quite different (Col. 3:5; Jas. 1:21; Phil. 1:27; 2 Cor. 1:12)?

Our first stage of transition was to adopt (or at least to allow, dependent on the conscience of the teacher) the New King James Version for use in the Sunday school. This needed careful management. Something of the background difficulty is indicated by the fact that about this time I received a letter from the deacon of another Strict Baptist church which began, rather ominously, with the words, 'It has come to our ears'. What had come to their ears was that we at Rehoboth, Coventry, were now using the NKJV in our Sunday school! When I confirmed that this was indeed the case, giving a few tentative reasons, the invitation for me to preach in that church was unceremoniously withdrawn.

It was actually thirteen years into my pastorate (1998) that we made the change from the AV to the NKJV as the recognised church Bible. While to many this will hardly seem to be a major transition, for Hazel and me, on both sides of our family there was a strong tradition of 'AV only' which made change in this area particularly painful. The same was true for a number of others in the church. Yet in an inner-city setting and with a growing diversity of people attending the church, including those for whom English was a second language, we came to believe that this was the least we could do for the sake of the people we wanted to reach with the gospel. The same principle of intelligibility that influenced us then has been instrumental in guiding further gospel-driven change since.

The change of Bible version was handled very carefully over a period of years, with a lot of prayer and study of the issue in pastor and deacons' meetings. It was considered in depth at whole day retreats, and eventually papers were brought to the members and time given for these to be absorbed and discussed.

The moment of breakthrough came in a questionnaire to church members on the subject, when it became evident that most of the families of the church were by that time using the NKJV or another version in their homes. The reality was that the majority were already making a sacrifice, accepting a different Bible version in the church to their preferred one at home. Was it now time for the minority to make the sacrifice the other way – to read their AV at home, bring it to church with them, but to accept that the version used publicly in the church would now be the NKJV? People were gracious and the change was finally made.

Singing God's praise

Throughout its history until the beginning of my pastorate, the church at Rehoboth had used the nineteenth-century selection of hymns already referred to, and known affectionately as *Gadsby's*. It is a somewhat strangely organised selection of over 1100 hymns. Some well-known hymns are omitted, curtailed or altered to reflect particular theological sensitivities. Authors, like Charles Wesley, whose theology was considered questionable in some aspects, are indicated only by initials rather than their full name! *Gadsby's* contains some real gems, but many of the hymns are more suitable for private meditation than public singing. The language is often quaint and the content introspective, and therefore hard for the uninitiated. The tradition in Gospel Standard churches is for the deacon to choose and announce these hymns, which are then sung, often unaccompanied, at a very measured pace. With some good singers, and in four-part harmony, this singing at its best can be reverent, joyful and quite impressive. But in declining congregations the story is often quite different. The singing of the praise of God had become gloomy, unmusical.

At Rehoboth we had a harmonium which had been fixed with a power supply so that pedalling was no longer necessary. It was not the most felicitous of instruments. When Hazel and I were married at the chapel in 1975 we made a request to bring in and use an electronic organ for that occasion only, but this was refused by the deacons in office at that time. Paradoxically, the subject of the singing of God's praise, and the type of accompaniment used, is often one of the most contentious and divisive in the life of a church.

We began, slowly and carefully, to address this issue. It seems hardly possible that anyone would object to words from the Bible itself set to music (yet some do) and we began judiciously to extend our repertoire of sung praise by use of these. When talks to the children were introduced in the Sunday morning service, they were often followed by a short Bible verse set to music, or by a song suitable for the children.

A few other Strict Baptist churches with which we were connected were also becoming dissatisfied with the exclusive use of *Gadsby's*, and eventually a supplement was produced, *Hymns for Worship*. It was never intended as a stand-alone hymnbook, but for Rehoboth it facilitated the gradual extension of our repertoire of items sung. This is another area in which change began slowly in those early years, and then, motivated by the principle of intelligibility, quickened its pace exponentially.

Rehoboth is possibly unique among churches to have graduated, in an act of ecclesiastical long jump, from *Gadsby's* to *Praise!*. At the same time, the use first of overheads, then of PowerPoint, enabled us still to use some of the old favourites plus many more modern compositions. Our standard was, and is, the biblical accuracy, excellence and content of the items sung, not their genre or theological stable of origin. Blessed with a gifted hymn writer in our own congregation, we have been able to continue to use some of the best in *Gadsby's* with some judicious alteration and updating. Though changes of this kind will no doubt remain contentious, being adaptable certainly eases transition.

Our motivation in the changes we have made in this area has been to try to ensure that our singing of God's praise is true to Scripture, but also intelligible and accessible both to churched and unchurched people. In other words, these changes were, in their intention, gospel-driven. We all need to be able to understand and relate to what we are singing. The praise of God needs to be done well and to his glory. Musical genre and accompaniment is bound to change from generation to generation.

Head coverings

In my first year as pastor, I had the temerity to preach from 1 Corinthians 11. I was brought up with this – that women should have their heads covered in public worship – and I still believed it. In 1985 all women members of the church complied with it and regular female members of the congregation and visitors were expected to comply. I was aware, however, that not all were convinced that this was a genuine biblical requirement for the twentieth century.

Nonetheless, in that year I preached that the principle of headship and submission outlined in 1 Corinthians 11 still needs to be symbolised by the wearing of a head covering by worshipping women. Over subsequent years this was repeatedly put to the test. God kept sending us people with a different conscience and practice on it – godly, Bible-believing people. Female students from different church backgrounds especially found the requirement difficult. More than once we had women visitors, not believers, whose first question after the service was not about the gospel, but about head coverings. The issue would not go away. It was becoming increasingly clear to me that, although I had made a public, pastoral ruling, my teaching on this issue had not been fully persuasive.

The desire grew within the church leadership to re-examine. Together we did some detailed work on the text of 1 Corinthians 11 – and a lot of heart searching. Eventually I made a statement to the church members that we now wished to make this a matter of Christian liberty to the women of the church, in consultation, where relevant, with their own husbands. I gave four main reasons:

1. That the passage teaches an abiding and unchanging principle – of headship and submission. There is order in the church in which roles are defined and the principle of submission must be worked out in the life of the church.

2. That the church in Corinth knew exactly what Paul meant when he wrote to them about a practical and visual way of showing this submission. The fact that we do not know shows that cultural realities are involved.

3. That the then universally recognised symbol of submission was most likely a veil that covered not only the hair but the whole head and face of the woman when she was in public. This was understood by people both outside and within the church. A woman without a veil in that society was making a statement about submission.

4. Experience has taught us that people today just do not understand what the wearing of head coverings is intended to signify.

This statement was given to the church in 1996. It had taken over ten years for the change to take place. During that time people had graciously adhered to the practice, amid a growing sense that it was indeed a potential stumbling block to people, especially women. If people are offended by the gospel itself, it is one thing: if they are offended or stumbled by a practice hard to explain and justify, it is another. After this, some women continued to wear a head covering but it was now a matter of conscience and by far the majority of women and girls in the church discontinued the practice.

Such changes in a church that belonged to a close-knit denomination with strongly uniform characteristics did not go without wider observation and criticism. With my Gospel Standard background, and family connections, and my continued occasional preaching in Gospel Standard churches, I suppose I was, in our church, the one most aware of this, and sensitive to it. It was a different issue, however, propelling itself into our church life, which brought about a change that would set the church on a different trajectory in its association life.

Communion

During 1991 one of the church families had a visitor from Russia who asked whether he could join with us at the Lord's Supper, at that time a separate gathering after the evening service on the first Sunday of the month. Visiting Christians needed to ask to join us or be invited to do so. In a brief conversation with this young man, I heard his testimony, learned that he had been baptised by immersion in his home church and was a member in good standing. He was of the same faith and order in every biblical sense, although he was not, of course, a member of a Gospel Standard church. (There are no such churches in Russia!)

What I did not know was that this man had also asked a neighbouring Gospel Standard church whether he could commune with them, and been refused on the grounds that he was not a member of a Gospel Standard church. When the deacon of that church found out that he had been received at the Lord's Table in our church, instead of taking the matter up first with us, he wrote to the central committee of the Gospel Standard. He complained of our action, arguing that it was incompatible for the two churches to be in the same denomination because our practice differed with regard to the Lord's Supper. The result of this was some protracted correspondence with the Gospel Standard committee, and an interview with a delegation from that committee (which included my own father to try to make it more persuasive). Finally, perhaps inevitably, we were removed from the Gospel Standard list of churches. We felt unable to yield on such a vital point of principle. This man was a brother in Christ, wanting simply to remember his Lord, as commanded, who had followed the biblical order as we taught it. On what legitimate grounds could we withhold communion from him, and others like him?

Being cast off from our denominational moorings, finalised in 1992, was a big turning point in the life of Rehoboth Chapel and in my own journey. After this, the pace of biblical reformation quickened significantly. Until then we had always been looking over our shoulder and wondering whether our attempts at biblical reformation would disrupt our historic association life. Now we had missed the mark, and there is truth in the old proverb that 'a miss is as good as a mile'. For me there were ramifications both in family and in the churches in which I had previously preached. Some pulpits were now closed to me – which helped me to focus more on the work at home.

To begin with, I think we felt somewhat isolated. A natural association would be with other reformed Baptist and Grace Baptist churches, but this was not our historic connection. We began to develop stronger relationships with likeminded churches locally, and with churches nationally which were on a similar trajectory and with which there was a connection through pulpit exchanges, student contacts and family relationships.

Women and prayer

Another issue that concerned us as church leaders for a number of years was the conduct of our prayer meetings. The practice in churches of our kind had always been for men only to be 'called on' to pray. The custom was for a man to be asked by the leader of the service to choose a hymn and then after it was sung, he would pray. The tendency was for some of these prayers to become rather sermonic, long and introspective. Audible prayer was certainly not open to all. The sisters, specifically, were excluded.

We were now exercised about opening up our prayer meetings for all to have the opportunity to pray along the model, as we understood it, of Acts 1:14, 'All these with one accord were devoting themselves to prayer, together with the women and Mary the mother of Jesus, and his brothers.' It is difficult to initiate change when a custom, and the assumptions and habits that go with it, are so deeply ingrained. To include women in the church's public prayer life was at the time a radical development. It was not going to be easy and there were different views within the diaconate.

By 1993 we had five deacons. I was the only elder. In this kind of set-up, the role of the deacon inevitably becomes somewhat merged with elder-type responsibilities. In pastor and deacons' meetings and retreats we prayed together and tried to work through some of the big issues. They were good times and God graciously preserved a spirit of love, unity and mutual respect among us. That does not mean to say we always agreed.

On this particular issue in our group of six we were split four to two in favour of women joining audibly in prayer in prayer meetings. We aimed always to bring a unanimous recommendation to the church, so had arrived at an impasse. Eventually, in a memorable meeting, one of the men who was against the proposal graciously suggested that we go by the majority view. I was reluctant to move forward without total agreement. The meeting ground to a halt. There was a long silence. Then the other deacon who had been opposed spoke, an older man well respected in the church. He suggested that we introduce the change but for a trial period. After some discussion as to how this could work, the suggestion was supported by the whole group, and so the way was paved to bring the matter to the church.[26]

In these kinds of ways, over the years, we have seen God's gracious overruling. Still, such changes needed a careful process of consultation and advance notice in the way proposals were brought to the members. We have learned not to spring a major issue or decision on a church meeting. People need time to reflect and consider.

There are also ways of easing transition for those who are finding it difficult. In this case we worked hard to help those who found the change uncomfortable. For example, during the trial period we kept the Sunday morning prayer meeting as one in which only men prayed audibly. Even with these efforts, this particular proposal did meet with some opposition, and as a result, one family left the church. I think this is the only time, in all the changes that have taken place, that someone left as a result of a specific change. Even in this case there were other distinct factors in this family leaving.

The cost was worth it. For twenty-five years now we have had the joy of men and women praying together in our times

---

26 We have since used trial periods on several occasions. See chapter 8: 'Trial Periods'.

of prayer. The prayer life of the church has become more a symphony than a succession of solo instruments.

In 1985 it was also proposed to hold a women's meeting in which women of the church and congregation could pray and study the Bible together. This was something, again completely new at that point in the life of the church, that has now happily continued to the present day.

Dress code

When I began my ministry, most of the men attending church wore suit and tie, and the women also dressed up. Now there is no dress code except, I hope, what conforms to biblical standards of modesty. The ideal, in my opinion, is not that everyone dresses down, creating a new conformity; rather that people should dress in what feels right for them, culturally and conscientiously, not drawing attention to themselves. In this way anyone who comes to church feels affirmed in what they are wearing, so long as it is modest and not saying 'Look at me! Here I am!'

As the church has become more multicultural there has been a growing need to be adaptable on issues such as dress, punctuality, customs and expectations at dedications, weddings and funerals. Many of our African brothers and sisters, for example, have high expectations around dedications. Relatives may travel from a considerable distance, people dress up, the baby may be wearing a special gown. Those leading the service at least need to be aware.

Fellowship with likeminded churches

The dislocation in our denominational association life prompted us to seek fellowship with likeminded churches in Coventry and district. I began to get to know some local pastors. We were blessed, and still are, with good men leading churches in the locality, strongly committed to the Bible as the Word of God and preaching the gospel.

At about this time, an overture from the 'Churches Together' movement in Coventry concentrated my mind on this issue. I knew that some churches in that grouping did not believe or preach the historic gospel of salvation by grace alone, through faith alone, in Christ alone. Unable to work with them, we also knew there were other local churches which took their stand unequivocally on the Bible as the Word of God and the gospel of grace. It seemed right to seek closer fellowship and to take our stand in the city together. So, the Coventry Evangelical Forum was born. Initially it was simply a group of local pastors meeting in my home to pray, discuss issues, and explore ways in which together we could promote the gospel in our city and district. As time went on, we were joined by other pastors and elders, from Rugby, Bulkington and Leamington for example. Various initiatives grew out of this including:

- an open air witness in the city precinct
- a joint meeting on a Saturday evening hosted by each church in turn
- a series of study courses addressing specific subjects
- helping each other with evangelism

- pulpit exchanges

Some wonderful friendships have grown out of this. The fraternal continues to meet.

If, like me, you face change with more than a modicum of self-doubt and questioning, it is wonderful to see the gracious provision and prodding of our God in that very process. The nearest gospel church to Rehoboth geographically was Hillfields Evangelical Baptist Church (HEBC), only a few streets away. This was a church which in the 1970s had come out of the Baptist Union for doctrinal reasons. It had a succession of godly pastors. Its pastor in the 1990s was a man who showed great sensitivity to our journey as a church. For example, the two churches began to hold occasional joint outreach prayer meetings. When these began, we at Rehoboth were still conducting our prayer meetings with only men praying. The practice at HEBC, at that point the stronger church numerically, was different. Yet when they joined us, led by their pastor, they adapted to us with grace and sensitivity. I quickly found that I was benefitting greatly, and learning much, from my brothers in the fraternal. In the particular relationships God gave within it, I can trace the kindness and providence of God. Our relationship with Hillfields Evangelical Baptist Church was later to develop in a most unexpected way. Our broader association life would also see development – first a natural gravitational pull to the group of churches known as Grace Baptist, then in addition and in more recent years membership of the FIEC (Fellowship of Independent Evangelical Churches).

Children's work

I began to be conscious of the work of God in my life when I was about eight years old. This has given me, perhaps, an enhanced sensitivity to God's dealings with children. When awakened by the Spirit of God they take in much more than we think. It is so important to encourage and include them.

Not long into my pastorate I began to do a children's talk in the service on a Sunday morning. Only those who have experienced the very solemn atmosphere of worship in a Gospel Standard chapel can fully appreciate how radical it felt to take a visual aid into the pulpit. Later, 'sermon searches' were introduced to help children follow the sermon. We wanted to encourage children to stay in the church for the sermon and listen to the Word of God with their parents.

For many years we had an afternoon Sunday School. This included a small number of children from church families and a larger group of children from the neighbourhood. In some ways this was an uneasy arrangement, there being a significant gap in Bible knowledge and family background between the two groups, but the work went on for many years, with wonderful commitment from the teachers. More recently, work among children has shifted to weekday evenings with different clubs for different age groups. All these ministries have gospel intent and focus as well as the social aspect.

We also introduced the practice of dedicating little ones in the service on a Sunday morning, holding them in our arms and praying for them and their parents. This gave opportunity over the years to give teaching to parents about bringing up their children 'in the discipline and instruction of the Lord' (Eph. 6:4). They were also occasions when we could explain believers' baptism and why we do not baptise infants. It has been a great joy over the years to see many of these children we prayed for coming to know the Lord, some at a very young age.

The question was then thrust upon us, should we baptise children? Some Baptist churches agree a minimum age limit, perhaps mid- to late-teens. We respect that, but if a child shows clear evidence of repentance toward God and faith in Jesus Christ and has a clear, if simple, testimony of God's work in heart and life, the parents also observing it and consenting (but not pushing), what biblical reason is there to withhold baptism from them? What about church membership? Our policy has been to welcome converted and baptised children into the membership of the church but without the expectation that they will attend church business meetings until the age of sixteen, or vote until eighteen. When church meetings are of a purely spiritual nature – to pray or hear a testimony – then the children are welcome to attend. Converted children surely belong within the family of God's people.

Again, this was an issue never faced by the church before. We consulted with others, sought advice, but our final touchstone must always be the Word of God itself.

Gradual growth in diversity

As we began to work through these issues, God gradually began to send us more people, and a more diverse mix. In the first ten years or so of my ministry there was a slow, steady trickle of conversions from within the congregation, and at the same time some significant changes in its demographic. For example, a couple of families of Caribbean background began to worship with us, and in 1990 we welcomed our first black member. In 1992 we saw the conversion of a man in his fifties from a nominal Roman Catholic background. A little later, a man who had struggled with addictions all his life was clearly saved. Some of these people brought with them challenging pastoral issues and a need for more round-the-clock pastoral care.

Prior to my ministry, year on year the church had warmly welcomed a small number of students from both Warwick and Coventry universities, myself among them. Every Sunday there was an invitation for them to have lunch and spend the day with a church family or individual. Coventry University, especially, was now growing rapidly through its policy of attracting international students. We found ourselves welcoming students from all over the world, to begin with in ones and twos, more recently in greater numbers. This development has been a source of great blessing and encouragement, some students staying on and serving in the church to the present day, others moving on into various spheres of Christian ministry, including at least four who have become pastors or elders of churches elsewhere.

An unexpected development in more recent years has been students visiting us who have never before stepped inside a Christian church. Many of them from China, they come out of curiosity, wanting to experience English and Christian culture, not appreciating that a church like ours is hardly fully representative. We have had the great joy of bringing the gospel to these people, sometimes across significant language challenges. In some cases, initial curiosity has turned into serious seeking and genuine conviction and conversion. These have returned home, taking the gospel with them, and often a Bible in their own language.[27]

Another development has been that some leaders of the university Christian Unions have chosen to attend the church, bringing a kind of recommendation, and further contacts. Invitations began to come in for me to speak at the local Christian Unions and this is now a regular occurrence with the current pastors.

There is no doubt that social and ethnic diversity within a congregation encourages more of the same. As people feel affirmed and welcomed, from whatever background, barriers are broken down. It is not uncommon now for us to have twenty or thirty nationalities represented on a Sunday morning, though there is still a deal of work to be done to integrate them fully into the life of the church. This is not easy where one culture has dominated for so long. To achieve anything like full representation of the ethnic and social diversity of our membership in our members' meetings, for example, is a long-term goal. For white British people, the way we do things in the administrative life of the church is second nature, but unfamiliar and strange to people from other cultures not so

---

27 See chapter 6: 'Slices of Life'.

bound by time or bureaucratic organisation.

Put yourself in the shoes of an African or Asian family worshipping regularly in an English church which is by degrees, and under the blessing of God, becoming more culturally diverse. More and more black and Asian people are joining the regular congregation. Some of these remain on the fringe: others become more involved. They are baptised, become members, but all the elders and deacons and home group leaders continue to be white and British. Rarely do you see on the platform someone of your own colour. You seldom hear a black or Asian preacher in your church. As time goes on, this situation surely calls for change. You would expect to see gifts develop and leaders of ministries emerge right across the board. It raises the question as to whether we could practise a kind of positive discrimination, a fast-track into leadership to reflect more accurately the ethnic diversity of the church and achieve greater cultural integration. At the very least, it seems to me that we should be vigilant for opportunities to appoint suitably gifted people as leaders of ministries, home group leaders, deacons and elders. This is an issue which we as a church are currently trying to address. If a more thorough integration can be achieved without compromise on biblical qualifications, this will surely be a happy and biblically wholesome development.

Certainly it is true to say that, in spite of the challenges of multicultural church life, such as we experience it, it is a wonderful foretaste of heaven.

Leaving the classroom

During the first four years of my pastoral ministry, 1985-89, I continued in my position as head of Religious Studies at King Henry VIII School in Coventry. Looking back on it I can scarcely believe that alongside this I was also preparing at least two sermons and one Bible study per week and leading the church. I remember dedicating Saturday afternoons as family time. I am afraid that my wife, always a stalwart support and indefatigable worker in the church, had rather a poor deal. I was trying to prepare two sermons on a Saturday morning and evening with some borrowed hours during the week. It was not sustainable long term. It happened because when I began as pastor, the church was still only small and there were those in the membership who were concerned, for my sake and my family's, about taking me out of employment. What if the church should decline? It was a real issue.

A couple of years into this period I shared my situation with the head teacher of the school and he kindly arranged for me to have one afternoon per week to devote to church work. I continued in my head of department role – an unusual arrangement facilitated by the fact that it was an independent school. In this I saw the clear hand of God, his gracious provision.

By 1989, however, it had become clear to me that I must resign my position at the school and devote myself to the pastorate. By this time, the church had grown sufficiently for things to look more promising. The school asked me whether I could continue to do some part-time teaching, which I did, on a small scale, for the next ten years. By the time I fully relinquished teaching we were getting ready as a church to employ a further full-time worker.

Chapter 4
Turning points

Although the pace of change was slow to begin with, gospel-driven change was happening. God gave us significant turning points. Some have already been mentioned – the early sermons about vision, and ejection from the denomination. There were others, which caused the pace to quicken.

Appointing elders

The model of leadership that most Baptist and Congregational churches above sixty years old inherited was of an ordained or recognised minister, supported by a diaconate. In larger churches the minister may have had an assistant or co-pastor, but the basic church structure was normally pastor and deacons. It had been the case at Rehoboth throughout its history. The result often was, as we have already seen, that the deacons functioned in an enhanced role to that defined in the New Testament.[28] In many churches, deacons were dealing

---

28 The New Testament pattern is for spiritual men to serve in practical ways, freeing up elders for prayer and Word ministry (Acts 6:1-7).

with eldership issues and doing eldership tasks. This was the case at Rehoboth. It was working well and in one sense there seemed no reason to disturb the pattern.

If, however, we are committed to biblical reformation, we surely have no option but to re-examine and reorder our practice, no matter how long-established or deep-rooted it is, or how well it is currently working. The biblical model for church life is undoubtedly a plural eldership where possible, with elders supported by deacons. It is not about hierarchy, but about function and service. All appointments to office in the church need carefully to avoid any suggestion that it is about status or position or power. We are not a worldly club.

In 2002 we appointed two additional elders and, as the church has grown, we have added further to the eldership and have seen how vital in a time of growth is the recognition of plural eldership.

Building project number one

Church buildings can easily be a sacred cow, especially where a church or chapel has history and tradition on its side. People become strangely attached to buildings, pulpits and (in hot weather, quite literally attached to) pews. We need a robust and biblical theology about our buildings.[29]

The Lower Ford Street building consisted of a simple Victorian chapel (built in 1857) and named Rehoboth by the people who first worshipped in it. They felt that the Lord had

---

29 See chapter 7: 'Entrenched attitudes'.

'made room' for them in this part of the city (Gen. 26:22). Apart from the chapel itself there was a small meeting room with facilities at the back, and a flat floored and boarded off gallery at the front. There were two small entrances with porches and green baize-covered inner doors and the chapel was filled with wooden pews. In a central elevated position was the pulpit.

In 1998 we embarked on our first major change to our building. At that stage there was no urgent need for extra space for the congregation, but we did need to provide ancillary rooms for smaller groups and teaching purposes. Our main concern was to improve the ambience and welcome of the building itself, which was, it has to be admitted, rather forbidding. New entrances had been installed some years before creating a more open space to welcome people. Now we removed all the pews and the pulpit, levelled the floor and turned the orientation ninety degrees so that the new platform, just one step up, was against the long wall and the new fabric chairs arranged in an arc or semi-circle. This, with attractive wall panelling, created a more inviting ambience to the whole chapel. From the preacher's perspective, the congregation was now much closer, and eye contact, and a sense of connection, more easily achieved.

Reflecting my own conservative approach to change, I was initially reluctant to part with my old pulpit, being in favour of integrating it somehow into the new design. Thankfully others could see that this could easily become a hotchpotch and one of the deacons had the foresight to remove the pulpit and store it in his garage at home until the work was completed. I have not seen it since!

We saw the Lord's provision, not only in providing the finances, which were relatively modest, but also in the provision of a family firm of builders whose managers were members of the church. They oversaw the whole project and enabled us to keep costs down with a lot of the detailed decorating work done by volunteers.

We would have been surprised at that time if we had been told that a growing congregation and its needs would, sixteen years later, be looking to a major re-design of the whole site.

I still remember, however, the quiet wonderment in a pastors' fraternal meeting when it was shared that we, historically the most conservative church in the group, had been able to remove our pulpit and pews with barely a ripple of opposition. We were helped by the fact that the chapel was never a listed building, never particularly beautiful, and the pews distinctly uncomfortable. Still, it seemed a bold step at the time, and I remember being absurdly grateful when an older Strict Baptist minister who had preached in the chapel in 'the old days', looking at the new arrangement, remarked with a twinkle, 'Well of course you know the Puritans preached along the long wall.'[30]

A legacy

Before I began my ministry, a church member left the residue

---

30 In a traditional Anglican parish church, the nave would have been long and narrow. The Puritan preachers turned the seats to face the long side wall, to gather the congregation around the preacher.

of her estate to the church. This was invested prudently and over the years accrued. As time went by, there was a growing sense of unease about simply sitting on this money and the conviction grew that we should use it to strengthen the evangelistic arm and outreach of the church. The vision was born for what we then called a 'city missionary'. The idea was to call another paid worker to help mobilise us in reaching out to our neighbourhood with the gospel. He would 'do the work of an evangelist' (2 Tim. 4:5). A job description was drawn up and we began to discuss this vision with several contacts we had which looked promising. These early efforts came to nothing but perhaps helped to crystallise our thinking.

I remember a particular church meeting late in 2000 when members were getting understandably restless about the fact that we were not using this money for gospel work. The suggestion was made that we advertise for the post in the Christian press. I was reluctant to do this, not wanting applicants to apply just for 'a job'. Having experienced a few closed doors, it seemed so vital to be guided clearly by God to the right person. We agreed to pray about it with a new sense of urgency. Little did we know that the answer would come within a few weeks, and that it would all hinge on a pair of shoes.

A pair of shoes

I had never had any formal training for ministry at Bible college. It is not expected, or provided for, in Gospel Standard churches where the emphasis is strongly on a personal call to preach and then dependence on the Holy Spirit. My first degree was a Bachelor of Education, taking Religious Studies as my main subject. The theology faculty I studied under was predominantly liberal – not the ideal training ground for gospel ministry. A lot of the challenge to me had been to try to debunk the higher critics.

I well remember a course on the atonement. All the major theories of the atonement were studied, but there was a strong prejudice against the substitutionary atoning work of Jesus Christ. We were told you cannot talk of blood sacrifice in the twentieth century. I wrote my end of semester essay in its defence – which seemed to cause a flurry in the department.

In the providence of God, I can now see these battles were a kind of preparation for what God knew was ahead. Coming from such a protected background, I needed to forge my own convictions. However, it was not a pathway I would commend to others.

In the year 2000, I had the opportunity to do a distance-learning MA in pastoral theology at the Evangelical Theological College of Wales, Bryntirion (now Union School of Theology). The opportunity, fifteen years into ministry, to study pastoral theology in a thoroughly biblical and evangelical setting was timely and helpful. The method was to work from home, but three times a year to do a residential week of quite intensive teaching and seminars at the college. I travelled with the pastor of a neighbouring church who was also on the course. At the college we shared a room. At the end of our first study week, we were sitting in the car ready for our return journey when my colleague realised he had left a pair of shoes in our room. I went to retrieve them. As I did so there was a young man in the corridor, a full-time student, just returning from the Christmas break. I paused on my errand for a brief chat. This was James Young. I asked him what his thoughts were about future ministry and he told me he felt his calling from God was to be an evangelist. He would love to work in a city. I asked if I could send him our job description, and we exchanged contacts. Thus began a fruitful and blessed ministry that has continued for twenty years to the present day.

When James finished his studies, he married Lis, so by the time they came to us we had two workers rather than one. Lis has been, and still is, an invaluable asset to the church, especially with her musical gifts and in her work among women.

There was the question of housing for James and Lis and the suggestion made that we should make enquiries about the three-storey terraced house next door to the chapel. Amazingly, in the providence of God, the owner was ready to sell and we were able to purchase and redevelop that property as a first home for James and Lis. Children began to arrive – eventually three – and so there was now a family on site. Later they needed more space and so moved out, and the first two floors were let to a Taiwanese family who attended the church. This building was later to be key in the redevelopment of the whole site.

When we first called James and Lis, we had sufficient funds to pay them for three years. In the amazing providence of God the support kept coming; and a couple of decades later they are still with us. Unsurprisingly, James' role in the church has developed through that time. To begin with, he operated as envisaged as a church worker, an evangelist, not doing the work for us but leading us in it. It soon became evident that with his preaching, teaching and pastoral gifts, James was also doing the work of an elder. In 2004 he was appointed an elder. Some years later he was formally recognised as one of the pastors of the church, so that by the time it came for me to give notice of retirement and a gradual scaling down of responsibilities, we were in the happy position of being able to appoint James as the lead elder.

A key retirement

A tremendous blessing and resource in church life can be released when a gifted man retires. In 2002 Peter Cordle retired from his work as Coventry City Treasurer. Peter and I had been appointed deacons of the church together in 1977. He had come to the church in 1966, three years before me. From the beginning, a strong David and Jonathan kind of friendship formed between us. Over the years Peter has been a loyal, wise and godly counsellor and encourager. He has always supported my ministry and role in the church humbly and wholeheartedly. I owe him an incalculable spiritual debt.

When Peter retired, he resolved to work full time for the church in an unpaid capacity, and has blessed the church with his particular gifts of administration and strategy as well as, with his wife Janet, gospel vision, pastoral care, hospitality and godly living. Year on year they have given freely and unstintingly of their time and energy. This, along with James' developing role, has given momentum to the reality that God has moved us away from a one-man to a team ministry. The development of a role for elders' wives has been another feature of this. They meet separately to pray and consider especially the support of women in the church.

In more recent years, the eldership has also been strengthened by the addition of others, two of whom are now serving the Lord in other churches (one as its pastor), and two who are still in the team, Dan Field joining us in 2014, Simon Hook as a co-pastor in 2019.

Chapter 5
A story of growth

Growth in numbers

By the late 1990s, nearly fifteen years into my ministry, we were feeling more ready to pray, 'Lord we've sought to prepare the spiritual nursery, please send the children', and our story since has, under the kind blessing of God, been one of growth. At the time of writing, numbers have shown a more than tenfold increase in both church membership and congregation since 1985, so that today we have significantly increased opportunities to bring the gospel to a wide-ranging diversity of people.

One aspect of the growth, admittedly, has been people joining us from other churches. This is not real growth in kingdom terms. If New Testament teaching was more lovingly and rigorously observed in churches, it would not occur. However, the church functions in a fallen world and is made up of fallen people. Things go wrong, people get hurt, a flock is not properly fed. A new beginning in another church is at times the best solution. Nonetheless it is also true to say of our church that many unchurched people are also coming within our orbit and are on our list of contacts.

Growth brings its problems and issues. How do you stay small and intimate while growing larger? How do you avoid the development of a large fringe of people who are only marginally involved? How do you reflect and integrate the diversity in church and congregation in the organic life and leadership of the church? Others have dealt helpfully with these, and other, very real issues associated with growth.[31]

Growth in ministries

Growth in numbers inevitably brings the need for more workers, more ministries. We now have many different clubs for children of various age groups in the church, as well as for mums and toddlers, for 18–30s, for retired people and so on, all with gospel intent. Small group and one-to-one Bible studies have also developed. All of this, together with practical tasks like cleaning, care of the buildings and administration, draws heavily on volunteers.

As the church has grown, we have also been blessed by the opportunity to take on church workers, often students who have stayed on to give a year, sometimes two, to the church when they have completed their studies. They volunteer in return for free accommodation and food. Some of these have continued to serve in the church, and have become full- or

---

31 See for example, Ray Evans, *Ready, Steady, Grow* (Nottingham: IVP, 2014).

part-time paid church workers. Others have gone on to Bible college and to further avenues of Christian service.

The welcome team

Crucial to the growth of the church has been our commitment to giving visitors and newcomers a warm and genuine welcome. The changes to the building have been very much with this in view. It is surprising what a difference the ambience of a building can make – and the right people in the welcome team. Our second building project has made the interface between the street and the church much more open and inviting. People can see through glass doors into the area we call 'The Link'. These doors are open on a Sunday and often one of the welcomers is out on the street. For many people, to step across the threshold of a church building is a scary thing to do. There is a degree of uncertainty as to what will be expected of them when they come in. It is so important to put them at ease, help them with practicalities, hand them a Bible and a notice sheet, tell them about the crèche and other provision for children where relevant, and show them to a seat.

We are an inner-city church and in the case of the Lower Ford Street building there are a lot of passers-by. The fact that they can see into the church and hear the singing as they pass by sometimes awakens their curiosity. We try always to be aware that there may well be someone in the church who is there for the first time and who has no knowledge of the Bible. The pastors always give a page reference to the Bible text and reading, and try to use language and concepts that are accessible. Thus we hope people get the message that it matters to us very much that they hear the good news of salvation. We are trying to say, 'We are glad to have you with us – to worship God, and to hear the gospel.'

A different mind-set

Connected with this, we found that we were needing to re-examine our habits, especially before a service. The tradition had been for everyone to come into the church building and settle down in a kind of sepulchral silence to prepare for worship. This, admittedly, is an attractive and worthy model. We were now beginning to find, however, that there were new people to meet and greet. It became common for people to arrive well after the service had begun. Things were not so tidy as they once were.

We began to encourage a different mind-set among our members – that we should aim to prepare for worship at home, but when we came to the building to make it our business to welcome people, and to expect a buzz of conversation in the chapel before the service begins. Long-held customs can be good, but can also be challenged if that is all they are. It takes grace to change with changing needs. Some people found it hard. One dear brother, now in glory, who used to pray very earnestly for the chapel to be full, actually found it quite difficult when his prayers were answered.

In many churches the custom is for the elders to pray in the 'vestry' before the service and then to make an entrance into the church just as the service is due to begin. Although prayer before worship is both desirable and essential, again it does not have to be done in that particular way – which has one or two distinct disadvantages. It takes the elders away from the people just at a time they can be pastoring the flock. We have found it very helpful as elders to meet and greet people in the half-hour or so leading up to worship. The practice of elders making an entrance can also communicate an unhelpful message about status. It would be interesting to know how the New Testament elders mingled among the people.

Hospitality

A further encouragement to growth in the church has been the enthusiastic development of hospitality both in the church and in people's homes. There is no doubt that people come together in a special way over food and drink. Providing hot and cold drinks and biscuits between the two morning services in church has been a great way for people to get to know each other. A shared simple buffet supper after the evening service, initially devised for students, has now broadened out in an invitation open to all. We have tried to resist the tendency for people to divide up into categories – students, young people, older people. It is good for people to know each other, and have fellowship with each other, across the different age groups.

Every few weeks we have a Sunday lunch together, the whole congregation invited. After the morning services the chairs are cleared and tables laid out in the main hall. Often a full hot meal has been served. Now, because of the numbers involved, it is more usually a meal of soup and dessert.

Evangelistic events organised by the church often include an element of eating together. Sharing food from different cultures is a rich way of expressing unity.

Many people in the church and congregation open up their homes – to people visiting on a Sunday, to students, to each other. A lot of this takes place over Sunday lunch. Students, especially, find it a blessing to spend Sunday with a Christian family or individual. They can also be linked up with church families for pastoral care and contact during the week. Several homes have also been available for people needing accommodation, either short or more long-term. Many have been helped in this way, and friendships formed.

The New Testament church was clearly a *community*. They met daily and shared their lives and possessions. In times like ours, when many people live dislocated, isolated lives, it is a blessing whenever the church comes close to being a genuine surrogate family. There is strong emphasis on the grace of hospitality in the New Testament (Rom. 12:13; 1 Tim. 3:2; Tit. 1:8; 1 Pet. 4:9). This presents a great challenge to churches today.

Perhaps the strongest single model of hospitality in church life is when a Christian couple adopts. This is permanent hospitality. One family in our church, having brought up four birth children, then adopted two more, one of them significantly disabled. There is real power in such visible examples of unconditional, and often severely tested, love.

Guest services

We have found the concept and practice of a guest service useful. It has pitfalls. Anyone should feel welcome at all our services. Do people invited to a special service tend to think that only that service is for them? If so, you get the syndrome of people who attend only once or twice a year at Christmas and Easter or harvest.

Even so, the evangelistic reach of a carol service, for example, can be significant. People have been saved through first attending just such an event. Sharing food together on these occasions can be helpful in building new relationships.

Home groups

One key way in which we have endeavoured to stay small while growing larger has been the development of home groups. These take place on alternate Tuesdays, the other Tuesday evening being dedicated to the whole church prayer meeting. These groups are small units normally of six-to-twelve people where the main emphasis is not so much on another meeting, but a gathering for mutual support, fellowship and prayer. The home groups have become a vital means for 'one another' ministry, of which so much is said in the New Testament. In small groups we are able to read the Bible, revisit the word preached on the previous Sunday, pray together and pastor one another.

Two morning services

The growth that was occurring began to test our capacity to accommodate the people in our chapel. The theory goes that when a church gets eighty per cent full it can become a disincentive for people to attend because of the difficulty of finding a suitable seat. We began to give serious thought and prayer as to how to resolve this. Church planting was a live issue, but there was no obvious area for us to plant into, and, rightly or wrongly, we did not feel that we could recognise sufficient people in the church with the gifting and calling for it. We conducted a serious search for a rented hall that could accommodate everyone on a Sunday morning. We considered the possibility of permanent relocation to different premises. In the end, however, the advantageous location of the Lower Ford Street chapel – on bus routes and with a good footfall – took us in the direction of planning for two morning services.

In some ways this was a clear example of growing pains. To many, the thought of dividing the morning congregation into two was disappointing, for some even questionable theologically. In addition, it was an arrangement that would require a lot more workers. Ministries needed to be doubled up – welcome teams and musicians for example. Yet we had to work within our physical constraints and to adapt quite quickly to changing circumstances.

Nonetheless, before we adopted the two-service model, we consulted with other churches that had done the same. This led to a firm decision that we would aim for two 'identical' services (the same preachers, Bible readings and hymns) rather than services of different kinds aimed at different target groups. Preserving unity and fellowship across all the different age- and preference-groupings in the church remained a vital aim.

So it was that in 2011 we moved to two morning services, at 09.30 and 11.30 with refreshments in between. In the actual practice of this, apart from the extra demands on people and the obvious toll on energy levels, especially of the preachers, we have learned that there are also undoubted benefits. The pastors are able to speak personally with many more people when there are two congregations rather than one. Visitors can be noticed and given a personal welcome more easily. More people's gifts are used. The sense of still being one church is strengthened by fellowship between the two services over tea and coffee. The evening service brings us together as one again. The prayer chain (a group email by which we share prayer requests and information across the whole congregation), the prayer meeting and home groups all help to foster the one-church reality.

Building project number two

It was also in 2011 that the church launched a major fund-raising appeal with the aim of a complete redevelopment of our church site. Our vision was to create a building with facilities to support our desire to serve our community and see the kingdom of God grow through people coming to Christ and Christians growing in maturity. The need now was for the whole space to become multifunctional. This required a decisive move away from the sanctuary concept for what had been the chapel. If you have the luxury of a separate church or sports hall perhaps this issue can be avoided. If you have, as we do, an inner-city site with no land round it, practicalities prevail. Is there any biblical reason why you should not serve a lunch or run a youth group in the same area that you meet to worship?

We created a second storey across the chapel building, utilising the empty space below the chapel's very high ceiling, thereby almost doubling the floor space. We also extended the ground floor meeting room to absorb the rear hall, and changed the point of entry to the other side. An inviting entrance lobby links to the house next door, and we have a lounge, offices and a purpose-built kitchen, as well as an upstairs hall, library and other ancillary rooms. The whole project cost around £900,000. At one point in the process of demolition and rebuilding only the foundations and rather forlorn shell of the Victorian chapel remained. Once again God provided the builders from within the church family and we saw his great kindness in the amazing way the finances came in.

Our first task in this project was to see if there was buy-in from our own congregation for the vision for this redevelopment. Our policy on church collections is normally low profile. We do not pass round a bag or plate but simply have boxes at the door marked for people's giving. We have never wanted to communicate to visitors any impression that we are after their money. Regular members of the church and congregation have nonetheless always given most generously,

A STORY OF GROWTH

many through the gift aid system. For this particular need, however, we dedicated two gift Sundays when there would be an open collection and people could make pledges and give towards the new building fund. On two Sundays in the autumn of 2012 we collected, or were promised, the awesome sum of £287,343 – a clear affirmation! In addition to this, £150,000 was offered as an interest free loan. An appeal was then made to other churches and Christian bodies and some grants were secured from secular organisations with the proviso that the new building be available also for community use, with appropriate safeguards. Remarkably, by the time the project was completed in July 2014 we had almost entirely cleared the outstanding debt. God had also provided the right people with the right gifts, especially our project manager, Peter Cordle, to see it through.

To begin with, we thought that the new hall would be able to accommodate us all, but it quickly became apparent that we would need to revert to the two-morning-service pattern. In view of the way this had become established prior to the new building, it did not seem a retrograde step.

The Link Café

Most of the grants from secular sources for the new build were conditional upon community use of the building – which was in any case part of our vision. To get people from the local community over the threshold of a non-conformist church is not easy. There are psychological barriers that do well to be broken down.

121

One of our main community projects is the Link Café, run by volunteers from the church, and open in the mornings on Mondays to Thursdays. It provides good quality coffee and home-made cakes, and other refreshments, at a very reasonable price, served via a hatch from the kitchen into the welcome area of the church.

Reference has already been made to Daybreak, a drop-in at church which ran for over twenty years. Over that time its clientele had become rather predictable and self-selecting. The vision now was to bring people from a wider social range into the church, and the introduction of modest charging and comfortable facilities has enabled this to take place. The Link is not overtly evangelistic, but all its staff are believers who try to reflect the love of Christ. Bible texts appear on a screen along with other information and it is easy for people to find out about various church activities. The Link also provides a great location for people from the congregation to meet, and invite their friends. Many a one-to-one takes place there.

Enfolding

The next development in gospel-driven change in the church was probably the most unexpected and unplanned of them all. Looking back on it now, we can clearly see how God himself opened the door.

While the Lower Ford Street building was being redeveloped the congregation needed to find a new home. This was generously provided by two local churches. For the fifteen months or so that our building was out of commission we worshipped over two services on a Sunday morning with our brothers and sisters at Hillfields Evangelical Baptist Church in Waterloo Street, less than ten minutes' walk from Lower Ford Street. In the evenings we were given the use of Durbar Avenue Evangelical Church which had its own service on a Sunday afternoon, making the building available for our use in the evening. The kindness and hospitality of these two churches was a wonderful expression of Christian fellowship and gospel co-operation. We could clearly see in it God's gracious provision.

While we were worshipping at Waterloo Street, we were invited to share the preaching and leading of worship with the Hillfields church. It was a time when the two congregations became much more closely entwined. There was a great sense of unity in the gospel, and harmony in sharing preachers and ministries across the two churches. It is interesting to reflect that Hillfields Evangelical Baptist Church had come out of a denomination (the Baptist Union) and Lower Ford Street Baptist Church had come out of a denomination (the Gospel Standard Strict Baptists) and now we were sharing almost identical church order and theology. The same fundamental truths were believed, the same gospel preached.

Waterloo Street, however, had for some time been in decline, despite being served by excellent lay ministry. When the time came for the Lower Ford Street congregation to relocate to its building, the Waterloo Street church was left more acutely aware of its need for revitalisation. In the ensuing couple of years strenuous efforts were made to seek a full-time pastor, but no agreed way forward was found. A retired pastor, Bernard Every, was asked to be the church's moderator, and this proved to be a significant development. After spending time with the church, Bernard felt he could see that a way forward for the Hillfields church might be a closer association with Lower Ford Street. An approach was made and a time of discussion and seeking the Lord's will began. There was a series of meetings between the elders of the two churches and a growing sense of fellowship and gospel purpose.

The Waterloo Street building is located in the heart of Hillfields, while the Lower Ford Street building is at the edge of it, closer to the city centre. For all these years we had been working as two separate churches more or less on the same patch. Now we could see that, in the circumstances, and with a united front, we could use these two buildings to bring the gospel to this needy area in a new way.

Very graciously the folk from Hillfields Evangelical Baptist Church accepted, even embraced, a process which, while it was taking place, we called enfolding. We were aware that a church merger could expend hours of time and effort in working out a new constitution and reconciling different ways of doing things in the two churches. The idea of enfolding, however, was simply for the one church to be enfolded by the other, such that Hillfields Evangelical Baptist Church would be absorbed into the Lower Ford Street Church. Its elders would cease to be elders, and its members would become members of Lower Ford Street. The one church would continue to operate under the constitution and leadership of the Lower

Ford Street Church. This took a lot of grace, but it has been truly remarkable how it has now taken place and, albeit with much prayer and effort, how smooth the transition has been. We are now one church with two sites though at the time of writing this concept is still being developed.

There has been a sense throughout the process that God himself is in it. Such a hard thing, humanly speaking, has happened, and so unplanned, that surely the great Head of the Church himself is behind it.

Changes of name

One change of church name in a single pastorate might be necessary, but two begins to look like carelessness! Yet in the providence of God two changes of name have seemed appropriate and wise during my ministry. As we have seen, the chapel was named 'Rehoboth' by those who built it, and for most of its history it has been identified by that name – though with several different pronunciations. Engraved in the stonework on the front elevation, the name will always be with us. Its difficulty is not only that few people can pronounce it, but also that virtually no unchurched person has the faintest idea what it means. Knocking on people's doors in the early days we found that some people thought it was a Welsh chapel, while others had scarcely noticed it. We wanted the chapel to become well known in the area and for people to know that they are welcome. We chose the cumbersome name, 'Lower Ford Street Baptist Church', because it simply locates what and where it is. We put

'WELCOME' in bold white lettering on the front elevation.

When we enfolded with Hillfields Evangelical Baptist Church we wanted to identify the enlarged church with its district – Hillfields. Our brothers and sisters at Hillfields Evangelical Baptist Church had also yielded up so much. It seemed good to preserve a sense of the identity of that church in the new name for one church with two sites – HCC, Hillfields Church Coventry. The decision to avoid historic defining labels not understood by many non-church people was deliberate.

Building project number three

Buildings are subservient to gospel purposes. The Waterloo Street church building was lovingly constructed mostly by its own members in the 1970s, some of them still with us. They have more reason than most to be attached to it and its accustomed use over the years. Yet they too have grasped the vision, that this building can now be used as a kind of headquarters for outreach into Hillfields.

At the time of writing, we are embarking on a third, this time more piecemeal, building project on the Waterloo Street site, aiming to improve and adapt it for future use. While the building work is being done, the main worship services are taking place at the Lower Ford Street site, though some ministries and activities continue at Waterloo Street.

We envisage that there will soon be capacity at that site for worship services as well as for other gospel initiatives. Already an evangelistic Sunday afternoon gathering has been launched – 'Open door at four' – to reach out to people particularly on the Hillfields estate. Provision is also being made to teach English to refugees and asylum seekers with the desire to share the gospel. It is important that the development of the building retains a strong degree of flexibility of use. There is no doubt that both its location in the heart of Hillfields, and its potential as a building, will give us many gospel opportunities, under the blessing of God.

Missionary links

Over the years, we have been able to develop and strengthen support of mission in various parts of the world. A connection with a group of churches near Oradea in Romania fostered a close relationship. For some years, a group of our young people joined a Romanian team to run camps for children, many from poor homes. We have also had missionary links with North Cyprus, Albania, Papua New Guinea, Morocco, the Philippines, Kazakhstan and Colombia, to name a few. Many of these are still ongoing.

One family in particular are our 'own' missionaries. Having worshipped with us as students, we supported them through Bible college, and commissioned them through their missionary organisation. Alex is a radio engineer and is enabling the development of indigenous Christian radio stations throughout sub-Saharan Africa. Mari is involved in a baby rescue service, caring for unwanted children, and ministry among women. They and their family were first based in Ghana, now in Cape Town. Several individuals and families from the church have visited them in both places.

Chapter 6
Slices of life

My aim in this chapter is to give an impressionistic view of pastoral life as I have experienced it in the last thirty-five years. Focussing on the unusual perhaps runs the risk of presenting a distorted picture. For most of the time the work of a pastor is the hard slog of preparing and preaching sermons, visiting and caring for the flock, conducting dedications, baptisms, weddings and funerals, and leading the church through the kind of issues I have been describing. The physical, emotional and spiritual commitment is enervating, and in a long pastorate, a long haul. Yet I have come to believe that, especially in city work, there are definite blessings attached to a long-term ministry. It can provide stability, not only for the church itself, but for the people whose lives it touches. It is surprising how often, after an interval of years, people pop up again, or re-connect with the church, sometimes with a rather bemused, 'Oh, are you still here?' The joy of serving the Lord among people you really grow to love is tangible. There is rarely a dull moment.

Tommy

Throughout my ministry we have had dealings with people with serious addictions – alcohol, gambling, pornography and the like. It is such a battleground, and none of us are above it. We are all broken sinners. We have seen lives redeemed and turned around by the power of the gospel. In some we have seen complete deliverance from an addiction. In others the battle continues to rage. Even where there is a genuine work of the Spirit of God, the work of sanctification can still be a rocky road. The damage caused in a life severely destabilised by an addiction goes deep. Some people we have known and loved, and had strong hopes that they are born again, have drifted away and today we do not know where they are, either spiritually or geographically. Yet the Lord knows and we rejoice that 'God's firm foundation stands, bearing this seal, "The Lord knows those who are his"' (2 Tim. 2:19). It is deeply humbling to see how God pursues his people by his amazing grace, and stays with them. If it were not so what hope would there be for any of us?

Tommy had an alcohol problem that, to my knowledge, he never fully conquered. I have no doubt he was a converted man. He once told me that they made too much of him when he was first saved. 'They had me on platforms giving my testimony – a man saved from drink,' he said. There is a deep lesson from this. We must never make personal trophies of people saved by the grace of God. We can always exalt the grace of God in a person's life, but must never do so in such a way that puffs up human pride.

When he was sober you could have real fellowship with Tommy. He loved the Lord; he loved the Bible. I have in my possession some treasured letters he wrote me. But, like others like him, when Tommy backslid, he backslid publicly. One Sunday he would be in church worshipping with us soberly and reverently, but very sadly there would be another when he would arrive under the influence of alcohol and create a scene. On one occasion he burst into the church while I was preaching and, until intercepted, began to harangue me from the bottom of the pulpit steps.

How do you deal with a man like this? I think the answer must be that you try to reflect what God does with sinners. He pursues us. I had a remarkable experience of this with Tommy. The time came when he moved away from Coventry to Northfield, a district of Birmingham. Perhaps inevitably we lost touch with him, but continued to hold him in our prayers. One morning I had a strong sense that I must go and look for Tommy. I could not get him out of my mind. In the end, I got into my car and drove into Northfield, praying that God would lead me to Tommy. It was a needle-in-a-haystack kind of search. I drove round the district for an hour or two, parking up in likely places and walking round, realising more and more that this was not a very rational scheme. Ready to give up and go home, I started to drive out of Northfield and there walking along the pavement, as large as life, was Tommy! He took me back to his place, where we opened the Bible together, talked and prayed. It was the last time I saw Tommy. I do not know whether he is still alive but I hope to see him in heaven if not before.

Heidi

Heidi, an effervescent young woman of great character and individuality, has been, and is, one of the great joys of my ministry. I well remember the day of her birth. I was called to the hospital, her parents still reeling from the shock that their first daughter (they already had two sons) had Down's Syndrome. I simply held her in my arms and loved her. In the first few weeks her life hung in the balance. She had leukaemia, a hole in the heart, and problems with her kidneys. When I visited her in Birmingham Children's Hospital, a little scrap of humanity, wired up to so many machines, it seemed impossible that she would survive.

She not only survived but thrived! You can read the story of her early life in *Surprise Package*,[32] an honest, engaging book about her by her parents. Since then, there have been some interesting developments in her life. The verse I gave to her family and church at her dedication has been very precious, 'They shall be mine, says the LORD of hosts, on the day that I make them my jewels' (Mal. 3:17, NKJV).

Heidi loves the Lord and has a remarkable understanding of the Bible and an encyclopaedic knowledge of hymns (as well as knowing the birthdays of everyone in church!). If you come as a visitor to HCC, Heidi is among the first people you will meet. She will quickly ascertain your birthday and tell you other people, famous and not-so-famous, with whom you

---

32 Steve and Liz Crowter, *Surprise Package* (Leominster: Day One Publications, first printed 2003, expanded edition 2008).

share it. She has a great gift for breaking the ice.

Heidi was baptised at the age of thirteen, a very joyous day in which because of her height we only needed about half the usual amount of water in the pool! Heidi is enthusiastic about many things, but she loves to be in church, worshipping God and singing his praises. Many of the hymns she knows by heart. She is our 'hymn monitor' and keeps a careful record of the hymns we sing to ensure that we do not repeat the same ones too often.

Heidi has now become a well-known and influential campaigner for people with disability. Her motto text is from Psalm 139:

> For you formed my inward parts; you knitted me together in my mother's womb. I praise you, for I am fearfully and wonderfully made. Wonderful are your works; my soul knows it very well. My frame was not hidden from you, when I was being made in secret, intricately woven in the depths of the earth. Your eyes saw my unformed substance: in your book were written, every one of them, the days that were formed for me, when as yet there was none of them. How precious to me are your thoughts, O God! How vast is the sum of them! If I would count them, they are more than the sand. I awake and I am still with you ... (Psalm 139:13-18).

Heidi has spoken in television and radio interviews, addressed government consultations, and spoken to gatherings of bishops in synod, always with her longsuffering but equally tenacious mother in support. In particular, she has been a champion of the 'don't screen us out' lobby, defending the right of babies with Down's Syndrome to be born and have a life. She has vigorously and, at times, eloquently opposed inequalities in the abortion laws that allow the abortions of babies with disabilities up to full term of a pregnancy. Heidi is a great believer in the sanctity of life: and the vibrancy and fullness of her own life is powerful testimony to it. At the time of writing, I have recently had the privilege of marrying Heidi to James, a fine young Christian man, also with Down's Syndrome. Their wedding, taking place on the very day when the most severe Covid-19 restrictions were lifted in July 2020, was witnessed by about thirty people in the church building, but the YouTube recording of it watched, I'm told, by over thirty thousand! All those people heard the gospel.

Small-mindedness

One Monday morning, quite early in the day, and early in my ministry, I had a phone call from an elderly man from the congregation who informed me in rather grave tones that he had suffered a sleepless night. I expressed sympathy and asked whether there was anything that he was particularly worried about. His answer was quite peremptory: 'Your tie.'

I struggled to remember the tie I had been wearing the previous day when I had preached, as usual, both morning and evening. He informed me that it was red. In point of fact, it was a fairly sober maroon. He told me that he thought that a black tie was much more suitable for a minister and quoted, 'holiness becometh thine house, O Lord, for ever' (Ps. 93:5, AV). Quite how he deduced from the Bible that black is the colour of holiness, he did not inform me. He also suggested that the colour of one's tie might betray one's political allegiance!

It was discouraging after a day of preaching God's Word that this was the issue. I guess my disappointment did show through in my suggestion that perhaps there were matters of greater importance to lose sleep over! Godly people do not always have godly concerns.

Big-heartedness

In ministry, and as pastors, we are often face to face with the deep mystery of God's providence. His ways are higher than ours; his thoughts higher than our thoughts. Ministering the Word of God when people are passing through profoundly perplexing experiences is a test of one's own faith, as well as the people's. Sometimes it is exceedingly difficult to face a Lord's Day when you know what some of the people are going through.

We have a man in our church who came to know the Lord relatively later in life. His wife was converted first and then we prayed for the husband for many years. When it happened, the change in him – the new joy he had – was visible to all. He had a friend, a doctor, with kidney failure. After prayer he felt it right, as an expression of Christian love to this man, to offer him one of his own kidneys. The match was good, the operation went ahead, there was much prayer about it in the church and ... after a few days, the transplanted kidney failed. The whole thing looked like a waste; a sacrifice too far. Besides, there would be a long-term impact on the donor's own health.

The thing that helped me through the first Sunday after it had happened, in the face of a deeply perplexed congregation, was that no one could take away the power of the action of the donor, and the love, the big-heartedness, of it. It was a kind of sample of the sacrificial love of Christ, except of course he sacrificed his all, his very life, and his sacrifice was completely effectual. Sometimes the sacrifices we make in his name seem to be just poured out like the water secured for David at great risk from Bethlehem's well (2 Sam. 23:13–17). Yet in it there is the sweet savour of Christ. The wonderful thing about handling the Word of God and the gospel of God is that there is always something there to encourage, to comfort and to challenge. I am convinced that the Word of God speaks into any and every situation you can get into in your life, or church life. We believe in the sufficiency of Scripture.

Ulterior motives

We have quite often had visitors to the church whose only interest was to get money from us, usually to feed a habit of some kind. I quickly learned that if someone sat down with me and started a long story, it was almost bound to end with a request for financial help. Early on we formed the policy that we would not in usual circumstances give people money, but would instead offer them some other material form of help – buy the ticket if they said they needed to travel, do a shop, buy a meal, a card for the gas meter, or a night's lodging. Quite often, it became apparent that they were not interested in these offers of practical help. On more than one occasion, I have bought someone a long-distance train or bus ticket, actually seen them off on the transport, and then seen them back in Coventry on the same day!

On occasions, the scam has been quite elaborate. In one, the perpetrator found out my address and called on us at home. He was a small ageing man of middle-eastern appearance. He told us that he was the pastor of a Strict Baptist church (he had done some homework) in Burma (probably not enough homework!) and that he had had to come to the UK to rescue his daughter from the 'clutches' of a 'suspect' Christian organisation. She had become friendly with a young man who was supposed to be a Christian and now she was pregnant. Our visitor only had the return fare to Burma for himself, though not enough to get his daughter home where she needed to be. He had Christian friends in Australia who had promised to underwrite the cost of the airfare, but they needed an English bank account into which to pay the money. He felt that the pastor of a church like ours would be trustworthy. He pleaded with us. There were tears. Could he use our bank account for this purpose? He suggested that we pray together about it. My wife and I have to admit that while he was 'praying' we both opened our eyes, looked at each other, and both understood the signal! When he had finished, I first offered to call his friends in Australia to confirm the story, but he said that they would be sleeping right now. Then I said I would like to meet his daughter and offered to go with him to do so. He said that she was not well and that was why she had not come with him. I told him that I did not find his story credible. It was a rather forlorn figure who sloped away from us that day. Should I have taken him to the police station? I do not know, but how sad that someone will try to play on Christian sympathies with that level of intrigue.

That man was completely unthreatening in his behaviour. Others have been more menacing. On one occasion I was just locking up the chapel on my own when a young man approached me with a request for money. He claimed to be a Christian from a Baptist church in Cornwall. He needed to get home, but did not have the money for the ticket. I told him what our policy was and offered to go with him to the bus station to buy his ticket 'home'. At that, he became aggressive. He accused me of not trusting a fellow Christian. Then he accused me of not believing the Bible. 'Didn't Jesus say "Give to the one who asks you"? I have chapter and verse,' he said. He got a Bible out of his rucksack and turned up Matthew 5.42, 'Give to the one who begs from you, and do not refuse the one who would borrow from you.' I explained that I was not refusing to help him but just choosing the method according to the policy of the church. He persisted in arguing that I would not do what he asked because I did not believe the Bible. 'So you won't mind if I tear that page out of the Bible will you?' he said. I told him I did not want him to do that, but doing it would not change our policy. Upon which he began to rip out page after page of his Bible, leaving it scattered all over the pavement. At one point I thought he was going to attack me. It was a disturbing, intimidating experience, but the Lord's help in such situations is very real.

A false allegation

For many years we ran an afternoon Sunday school. A minibus and private cars picked up the children to bring them in. Many of them were from broken homes and some of their parents were going through multiple relationships. These children were growing up in a highly charged, often sexualised, atmosphere. The mother of one of our regular families had many partners and was currently in a lesbian relationship.

My wife, Hazel, having served Sunday lunch to the family, usually including students and other guests, would then do a car journey to pick up children for Sunday school. The classes were spread round the building in various rooms and corners of the chapel. Hazel taught one of these groups.

One Sunday I had a phone call shortly after Sunday school had finished from the father of one of the children. He was very angry, claiming that my wife had interfered with his daughter, touching her inappropriately. He had reported the matter to the police. Poor Hazel had to return from Sunday school to be confronted with this news. Somehow, we managed to carry on with our family and church responsibilities that evening, under the threat of a police investigation.

A few days later, Hazel was preparing her next Sunday school lesson about Hannah in distress pouring out her heart to the Lord, and fully identifying with her, when two police officers knocked on the door. Their opening gambit was, 'We haven't come to arrest you.'

This was before the days when every church had very careful safeguarding policies. Thankfully, in God's kind providence, another adult had been present in Hazel's class that day and he had witnessed the entire lesson. The police officers said that they needed to speak to him and to other children in the class.

The police investigation came to nothing. The children in the class had all been at close quarters with each other throughout the lesson and no one had seen anything. At no point was Hazel alone with the girl. The girl herself however had stuck to her story, and it was very unpleasant having to live with the question – who would be believed?

As it happened, some years later I resumed visiting the family that had made the allegation and eventually the father apologised and admitted that it had all been a fabrication.

Weeks before this event Hazel had been praying that the Lord would help her understand what the apostle Paul meant when he wrote about 'the fellowship of his sufferings'. During and after this we understood a little more.

George

Late one Sunday evening, having preached morning and evening and feeling ready for a rest, I had a phone call from George who told me he was very ill and dying. George was another man with a drink problem who attended church regularly. The church had shown him great kindness.

When I arrived that evening, at his room in a block of flats, I found him in bed in quite squalid surroundings. He was never the picture of health, having a gaunt frame and poor complexion. On that evening, in those surroundings, he did indeed look as if he might be seriously ill. We talked. I read the Bible to him and prayed. When I opened my eyes he said, 'There is one thing you could do for me, I could really do with some fish and chips.' The whole episode had been about getting a free meal. A full Sunday thus ended down the chippy!

The man no one could help

One Sunday a man came into church in a very agitated state of mind. No one could do anything with him to calm him or alleviate his distress. My efforts only seemed to agitate him more. In the end I asked one of the older men in the church whether he might talk with him. This was one of our deacons, a man with a very gracious and gentle manner, who had experience of mental health crisis in his own family. The two of them disappeared into the vestry, and after about fifteen minutes came out, the troubled man like a lamb. He had agreed that he needed to check himself in to the hospital's mental health unit and that one of us could take him there.

I firmly believe that God gives to his church such gifts that are needed in any crisis, but it is certainly not the case that all those gifts reside in one person.

The man who said he was perfect

A man came into Daybreak, our drop-in, one Tuesday. He said he was a Christian, but in the course of conversation told us that he had now achieved a state of perfect sanctification. We opened the Bible and turned to 1 John and tried gently to show him that his understanding of things was not biblical.

Daybreak that morning was as usual a mixed group of people. Some of the regulars were there, not believers; yet all except the man himself could see he was under some kind of delusion. In the end, as the discussion got a bit more vigorous, the man lost his cool, and stormed out, in that very action and demeanour rather giving the lie to his claim. The Daybreak people never forgot this and talked about it often afterwards.

Harold

Harold was one of our Daybreak regulars. He lived in a hostel for homeless men. I am not sure that he ever learned to read properly, a fact he tried to disguise. He came every week and drank lots of coffee and ate lots of biscuits. He enjoyed the company, but his mentality seemed mostly to be one of 'take'.

However, during the period of our main building project there were three separate occasions when on arrival at Daybreak he gestured to me conspiratorially to indicate that he wanted a private word. On retreating to my study, he dived into his coat pocket and retrieved a bundle of £20 notes. Rather gruffly he said, 'I don't need this, have it for the church building.' When I counted up on two occasions there was £1000, on the other £2000! He was evidently living well below the level of his benefits. Thus the Lord raised up generous support for our building project from a most unexpected quarter.

Harold never said much, or showed much, by way of appreciation, but this was undoubtedly his way of expressing himself in friendship, and in support for the work of the church. Very thankfully, right at the end of his life he gave evidence that there was something deeper. The time came when he was admitted to hospital, terminally ill. I visited him and waited for a few moments as the curtain was drawn round the bed. When it was drawn back, Harold looked directly at me and said, 'You're the man I want to see.' He wanted me to tell him how he could be right with God. We had spoken to him many times about Christ, but this time I had the joy of leading him to the Saviour.

Asylum seekers

There was a Christian couple in London who had a particular burden for the many asylum seekers who were arriving in holding facilities, many of them from Iran. The husband, John, visited these men, mostly Muslims, in the hostel and invited them to their church and home. They usually had only a small window of opportunity because the asylum seekers were soon moved on to different parts of the country. So it was that I received a phone call from John to tell me that two of these men had been relocated to Coventry. He gave me their address and asked whether I would visit them.

These two were eager to learn English and study the Bible. They began to come to church and I started Bible studies with them, extremely basic to begin with as their English was so limited. The spiritual issues were complicated by the fact that these asylum seekers needed to develop a case to show that it would be unsafe for them to be returned home. One such case could be that they had converted away from Islam which meant that great care was needed in trying to discern motives. But here there was genuine interest, and a lot of questions. The time came when I was convinced that there had been a real spiritual awakening in these two. I then became involved in the legal proceedings especially for one of them, who decided also to change his name from Mohammed to Andy. Eventually they were baptised. One of them is still walking with the Lord today; the other, sadly, has drifted away.

An interesting development for the one who stayed is that one day I got a phone call from his solicitor to say that she had another client in similar circumstances, a young woman, and was it all right for her to recommend her to come to our church? Well of course it was all right, and that lady is now Andy's wife! How graciously God provides for his people. I married the couple, and the solicitor was present at the wedding.

On several occasions I have found myself in a court room dealing with applications for asylum, testifying that someone has now become a Christian, and it would be unsafe for them to be returned home. On one of these occasions, at a hearing in Walsall, the presiding magistrate asked me an interesting question:

'Is it not correct to say that Christians should be willing to die for their faith? Why are you then saying that this man should not return home because he may be killed?'

I must say I was taken aback by the question. However, the answer I gave was that, in the New Testament, it is usually the leaders or apostles who are the martyrs. You do not put a new Christian in that kind of situation. Whether it was that argument or another one that prevailed I do not know, but permission to stay was granted.

Out of weakness made strong

I have strong empathy with people who suffer from nerves in public ministry, having done so myself all my life. Samson is not often a good role model, but surely he has something to teach us when he cries out to God at his greatest point of weakness, 'O Lord GOD, please remember me and please strengthen me only this once, O God' (Judg. 16:28). Repeatedly I find myself saying to God, 'Please help me just one more time.' He is very patient. The only way really to take our attempts to serve our Lord is one at a time. Like the men and women of faith in Hebrews 11 it is 'out of weakness made strong'. By such means we are prevented from slipping into professionalism.

Some years ago, a student attended our church who volunteered to join the evangelistic visitation team. When it came to it, she was visibly nervous. She knocked on a door in Lower Ford Street. A rather alternative-looking young man answered it and she stammered out a few sentences, then re-joined other members of the team hovering nearby. After he had closed the door the young man said to himself, 'That girl was really nervous, she didn't have to do that: yet she still did it. Something real must have been driving her.' He decided there and then that he would go to her church and find out more. That man is today serving the Lord in pastoral ministry.

A visiting lecturer

Mention has been made of the many international students including visiting lecturers that come to Coventry University, some of whom have visited our church on a Sunday, mainly out of curiosity.

One day a relative of one of our members was out for a walk with a child, when a man asked her for directions. They got talking and he told her he was a visiting lecturer from China at Coventry University. Sensing an opportunity, she told him about our church very near to the university. His response was immediate, 'Can I come?'

A warm invitation and contact number was given, and the next Sunday this man was in church. From the beginning he drank in the message of salvation. In the first few weeks of his interest in Christianity, God brought him into contact with Christians in remarkable ways. At Christmas, he and his wife decided to visit London by train, but missed the last train home.

By an amazing chain of events, and with help from complete strangers, they ended up at a conference for Chinese Christians in Milton Keynes. God clearly wanted to ground him in the faith from the beginning. This man became a very dear brother in the Lord, and we had the great joy of baptising him before his return to China. Now various members of the church keep in touch with him.

There have been others like him, whose first interest in

Christian things was simply to come to church to see what it was like, and who have come to know the Lord, returning home as ambassadors for Christ. May there be many more! It would also be wonderful to see a similar interest in, and receptivity to, the things of God among Hillfields' more permanent residents. We must never lose sight of the fact that God can do that too.

No greater joy

In any ministry, there are setbacks and discouragements, long swathes of time when it seems little is being achieved. In my ministry, conversions have been relatively few and far between: but there is no greater joy in a pastor's life than to see people coming to know Christ and walking in the truth. Among many other tokens of God's grace and kindness, I have seen all three of our own children become believers and going on with the Lord. I had the joy of baptising each of them – and more recently one of my grandsons too.

I think of a lad sent to Sunday school at age four who in his teens confessed Christ; and of a nominal Roman Catholic who came to faith after I visited his son in prison. I think of a girl in my wife's Sunday school class saying she wanted to be a missionary, then fulfilling that ambition as she grew in faith and years. I think of boys we prayed for, and dedicated to the Lord, becoming elders of churches and able preachers of the gospel. I think of students who attended the church while at university going on to serve the Lord, some continuing at HCC, others becoming relay workers, staff workers, elders and pastors in other churches. I think of atheists, agnostics, followers of other religions becoming Christians – only a handful, but what joy! I think of faithful, gospel-hearted men and women ready to carry on the work as I step back.

Section Two:
Navigating gospel-driven change

Chapter 7
Identifying biblical principles

The gospel-driven change that needs to take place in your church, in another context, is probably quite different from some of the changes with which we have grappled at Hillfields Church Coventry. Yet it is more than possible that you do need to give thought to how people are greeted and welcomed in your church, or how to avoid a clique mentality. It is very likely that you need to consider how accessible is the language you use in church. How well can a warehouse operative or someone who speaks English as a second language cope with it? Single culture dominance may be a reality, and anything like full integration still a long way off. It may well be helpful to consider how you are doing on a grace versus performance trajectory. Underlying attitudes to attendance, punctuality, dress and non-moral behavioural issues may need to be challenged and revised. Is gossip a problem? Big change may be on the horizon in your church denomination or association, due to proposals and developments which threaten to compromise the gospel itself. The change attendant on confronting these, and other, issues needs somehow to be navigated.

Nowhere am I suggesting that God cannot work without such change. He is sovereign and mighty, well able to overcome all our obstacles and impediments. In his grace, he works in spite of us, not because of us. Nonetheless, we do still bear a responsibility to remove barriers which we ourselves may put in the way of people hearing and receiving the gospel message. We must do this in faith and with real gospel intent, not to labour to remove the offence of the gospel itself, but to deal purposefully with unnecessary stumbling blocks.

Looking back on it, I do not feel that the change that we have lived through at HCC has been handled particularly strategically or self-consciously. No doubt many mistakes have been made along the way. For myself, I know that the extent of my emotional attachment to the work of the church has at times resulted in me taking it too personally when people take up a different stance or viewpoint from my own. Together, I think we have got it wrong more than once in our pathway towards cultural integration. We were slow to notice, for example, that when we were cooking and serving a church lunch, the team was not representative of the ethnic diversity of our congregation. We are not a model for other churches. When we have got things right for us, it does not necessarily mean it is the right pathway for others. We are still nowhere near where we ought to be as a church of our Lord Jesus Christ. Yet we have been able to move forward unitedly on a whole range of fronts and this, I believe, is a mark of God's kindness towards us. We have learned lessons from the process that can surely be of help to other churches and their leaders. This chapter is an attempt to distil some of those lessons.

Spiritual realities

I am convinced that God does not bless a church, or cause it to grow, therefore, *because* it has the right strategies and policies or because it has the right leaders in place. Neither is it the case that simply because a church has grown, or been blessed by God, that this provides justification for its methods, or proves it is on the right track. The only ultimate reason a church grows in its impact with the gospel of Christ is because God is being good to it. Church pride is a disaster zone, as is trust in men or methodology.

Equally, change in church life can never be justified along the lines that this is what other churches are doing – or not doing. All our practice needs to be tested by the Word of God and bathed in prayer. The fundamental spiritual reality is that Jesus Christ is head of his church. This is true universally and locally. If a local church is truly to be a visible manifestation of the body of Christ in a given place it must consciously be under the rule of Christ. Tradition must not rule, but neither must the latest fad or fashion. Carelessly we talk about 'our church', but must never let such language hoodwink us into thinking it *is* ours. The only thing that really matters in the church is for the will of the Lord Jesus to be done. If all its leaders and members were to approach church life in such a spirit, our churches would be in a different place: all the change that takes place in them would indeed be gospel-driven.

We can never over-emphasise the need for prayer. Prayer, like sanctification, is about change. If we do not want to change, why would we pray? The early church was a praying church. They prayed before Pentecost and the blessing came. They prayed 'with one accord', unitedly (Acts 1:14). They continued to pray when the blessing came: 'they devoted themselves to the apostles' doctrine and the fellowship, to the breaking of bread and the prayers' (Acts 2:42). They prayed when trouble and opposition came: 'and when they had prayed, the place in which they were gathered together was shaken, and they were all filled with the Holy Spirit ...' (Acts 4:31). Prayer is vital to growth and vital to managing change in church life. The underlying and overarching prayer? 'Lord, may your will be done.'

When a church is facing change that is difficult to manage, or threatening to divide it, its leaders could do no better than to call for a special time of prayer (perhaps fasting too).[33] United prayer is powerful and precious. The Scriptures abound with urgent prayer: 'Let your work be shown to your servants and your glorious power to their children' (Ps. 90.16); 'Oh that you would rend the heavens and come down, that the mountains might quake at your presence' (Is. 64:1). Such prayer for revival is, by definition, prayer for growth with all its attendant change.

There have been times in our church life, in some of the

---

33 When the work at Rehoboth was still very much a 'day of small things' (Zech. 4:10), we practiced fasting in connection with times of prayer for revival, and this continues to feature from time to time in the prayer life of the church and its leaders.

changes described, that the anticipated change, and its potential for division, has loomed like a mountain. But we have prayed, and when we have come right up to the 'mountain' we have seen it quaking! Regular, sustained, united prayer for revival, for conversions, for God's guidance and providential overruling is a church's true power-house. The cliché is true – when God's people pray together, they stay together. In a less well-known hymn of John Newton's he has the lines: 'The force of their united cries no power can long withstand'.[34]

For several years we have held an early morning prayer meeting once a month on a Friday to pray specifically for revival. Here, and in all the prayer life of the church, we are regularly expressing our complete dependence on the power that comes from God alone. Our reliance is not on the measures that we feel impelled to put in place, but on the vital, powerful work of the Holy Spirit. He alone can revive and bless us. He alone can bring people from spiritual death to spiritual life.

If corporate prayer, under the blessing of God, is powerful, so too is the intercession of individuals. Who can estimate the value to a church of just one godly, praying person? Before my time as pastor at Rehoboth, one of its godly members found she could scarcely go about her daily work because she was so burdened in prayer for the spiritual welfare of a particular person. In the end she felt compelled to ask other members to join her in prayer in her own home. Wonderfully within a

---

34 From the John Newton hymn 'Happy are they to whom the Lord his gracious name makes known'.

few days the prayers were answered. That person, held back for years through lack of assurance about his salvation, came forward for baptism.

Fundamentally, in managing gospel-driven change we need God himself. We need the grace of God to be upon us all.

Alongside utter dependence on God, we also need the distinct strategies that go with true gospel intent. New Testament examples of this are:

- Barnabas' strategy to fetch Paul to Antioch to join him in teaching new Christians (Acts 11:19-26).
- Their strategy to preach first in synagogues to those who knew the Old Testament Scriptures, and then, upon rejection, to turn to the Gentiles (Acts 13:46-47).
- Paul's preaching strategy in Athens, using pagan poets as his starting point (Acts 17:16-34).

Working through gospel-driven change is essentially a *spiritual*, not a pragmatic or prudential exercise. It is about seeking the will of the Lord Jesus Christ and submitting to it. It is hard to envisage that change will ever take place, especially in a church with a long tradition, if there is little or no sense of gospel purpose, or of collectively saying; 'Lord, what do you want us to do?'

Further, it must be evident that true gospel-driven change must come about by preaching and believing the Word of God. It is not only that change must always come under

Bible scrutiny: it must be prompted and fashioned by the Bible. When we read, for example, that Jesus was moved with compassion when he saw the vast crowds of people like sheep without a shepherd (Mk. 6:34), we are surely justified in asking questions. Indeed, we should be compelled to ask them:

- Are people today like sheep without a shepherd?
- Do I/we need more compassion for them?
- What would more compassion for the lost look like in my life? In our local church?
- Are there unwarranted barriers in our church to the lost hearing the gospel?

The best change thus results from true biblical conviction. A church committed to regular, systematic Bible preaching and teaching is bound to change for good – reformed and always reforming. Pastors and preachers must not evade passages in the Bible that may challenge existing emphases, beliefs, traditions or practices. When people see that change is genuinely Bible-led and gospel-driven, they catch the vision.

Reassurance

Change, as we have seen, is often painful. It can be more painful for church leaders than for anyone else. It is the calling of leaders to provide reassurance both for the flock and for themselves. Of course, this is to be found in God's Word and promises; in his assured presence with his people. It makes such a difference where there is genuine trust; where all trust God, the people trust their leaders, and the leaders trust their fellow-leaders. What can be more encouraging than Christ's words to his disciples as he gave them the Great Commission, 'And behold I am with you always, to the end of the age' (Matt. 28:20)?

Reassurance at times of change can also come by showing that the vital things are even more firmly in place, the things most surely believed among us (Lk. 1:1, AV). We need to strengthen the tent pegs at the same time as we lengthen the guy ropes to remind ourselves of the things that are unchanging. God himself never changes. Jesus Christ is the same yesterday, today and forever. He is the Rock of Ages. The promises of God are always 'yes' and 'Amen' in Christ. Heaven and earth may pass away but the Word of the Lord stands forever.

Comfort zones challenged

If we are genuinely committed to gospel-driven change, it cannot all be reassurance. The reassurance must come *with* the change, not instead of it. If our Saviour left the comfort and glory of heaven and made himself of no reputation to take the form of a servant among us, it is not surprising if we in his church are called to have the same mind, to walk the same kind of road (Phil. 2:4–11).

The regular, systematic preaching of God's Word is bound to lead us out of our comfort zones. Sometimes it is helpful for the whole church to consolidate and take stock of the teaching we have received. One such opportunity for us as a church has been our bi-annual church holiday. For the first few of these we did the teaching in-house. One year the theme was the difference between a community based on grace, and one based on performance. In this we were helped by a paper given by Tim Chester.[35] Some of the contrasts we considered were:

- About grace itself: do we talk about grace but actually communicate legalism?
- About the gospel: do we show that believers continue to need the gospel as well as unbelievers?
- About actions: are they driven by duty or by joy?
- About leaders: do the church leaders appear self-conscious of authority?
- About identity: do we find our identity in our ministries or in Christ?
- About failure: do we find failure devastating or are we able to live with it?
- About conflict: is it suppressed or addressed?
- About our conversations: do people speak well of each other or are they gossipy and critical?
- About brokenness: are we prepared to live with a degree of messiness and brokenness within our community or are things 'swept under the carpet' to maintain a sense of respectability?

35 Evangelists Conference, October 2008.

- About diversity: does the church appeal more to a certain type of people (e.g. middle class or white people) or to all?

- About converts: is the church ready to receive new converts or are there significant barriers?

All of this is deeply challenging, but the bottom line for each of us is surely our own brokenness and need of grace. How could we ever lift ourselves above the broken people round us? If the apostle Paul, always so conscious of his past way of life, described himself as 'less than the least' (Eph. 3:8, NKJV), and 'the chief of sinners' (1 Tim. 1:15, NKJV), how could I behave as if I am on a higher plane?

Entrenched attitudes

One of the most persistent obstacles I know to a church making genuine progress in gospel-driven change is our tendency to cling to deeply ingrained habits and presuppositions. We often do this without even being aware. We have caught the language forms of our forebears, and inherited their attitudes and practices. Where these are not properly biblically rooted, the only way to deal with them is again by patient and consistent Bible teaching. We need to take a long-term view. Some attitudes are so residual that they take a lot of shifting.

One example is our belief and practice around our use of church buildings. Without changes of attitude on this front at HCC, we never could have made the progress we have in using our buildings creatively for gospel purposes. Reaching and serving people needs to have priority over being precious about a building. It may be different for those churches that have, in addition to what they term the 'sanctuary', capacious church halls and grounds for other uses. But those, like ourselves, with more limited facilities are forced to think the issue through. Churches that meet in schools and other multifunctional spaces have already had to confront the reality that their worship space is not set apart only for that purpose. The previous day it may have been a venue for yoga, wine-tasting or bingo!

The traditional view is that the chapel or church building is itself in some way a holy place, a sanctuary, dedicated for worship. This attitude surfaces across the denominations, but is perhaps the more surprising within non-conformity where so little emphasis is placed on architecture or aesthetics in the building. Theologically, the sacredness is understood to be not in the place but in the presence of Christ with his people (Matt. 18:20), yet still our people pray about the joy of being in the 'house of God', meaning not the assembly of the people, but the building itself. One of my sons was told off by an older member of the Rehoboth congregation for being on the pulpit steps after a service. Once I preached in a Strict Baptist chapel where the previous Sunday there had been a row about someone putting a cardigan on the communion table!

The confusion arises from applying Old Testament practice to New Testament times. The tabernacle and the temple were places where God especially manifested his presence, such that the godly in Israel had an authentic regard for the place where God revealed his glory. When Solomon dedicated the temple, 'the glory of the LORD filled the house of the LORD' (1 Kgs. 8:11). The Psalmist longed for 'the courts of the Lord' and said he would 'rather be a doorkeeper in the house of my God than dwell in the tents of wickedness' (Ps. 84: 2, 10). Yet even in the Old Testament there are strong indications that such buildings are temporary, and that God is not confined to time or place. Abraham built an altar in every place he settled, an indication that the altar was truly in his heart. We hear God saying, 'Heaven is my throne, and the earth is my footstool; what is the house that you would build for me, and what is the place of my rest?' (Is. 66:1). The deeper prophetic insight is that God himself is the sanctuary (Ezek. 11:16).

The New Testament sees a radical departure in fulfilment of the true Old Testament vision. Imagine the horror of the priests who were serving in the temple on the day that the veil separating the Holy of Holies from the Holy Place was rent in two from top to bottom (Matt. 27:51). It was an act they would regard as sacrilege. Yet God himself did it. The temple, soon to be razed to the ground, was no longer the place where God manifested his glory. The glory was now revealed in the Word made flesh, and in the connection of believers to him, who would themselves, astonishingly, be the temple of the Holy Spirit (Jn. 1:14; 1 Cor. 6:19). Behaviour in our relationships with one another is what Paul envisages when he writes to Timothy about 'how we ought to behave in the household of God' (1 Tim. 3:15).[36] It is not unknown for people who claim to be

36 'House of God' in AV and therefore more open to misunderstanding,

believers to behave impeccably in church or chapel, only then to be disruptive in their relationships with fellow Christians.

There is no evidence whatever, beyond very early meetings in temple and synagogue, that the New Testament church met in dedicated buildings. They certainly did not have a buildings-based approach to evangelism. The apostolic policy was to begin in the synagogues where there was a ready-made congregation. Fearlessly preaching that Jesus is the Christ, they were soon ejected. In Corinth, they decamped to the house of Titius Justus who lived next door to the synagogue (Acts 18:7). In Ephesus, they used the hall of Tyrannus (Acts. 19:9–10). In Troas, Paul preached in an upper room (Acts 20:8). In Athens it was in the open air (Acts 17:22f). The default was to meet in people's homes (Acts 2:2,46; 5:42; 8:3; 16:15; 20:20; Rom. 16:5; Col. 4:15; Phlm. 2).

All these facilities were multifunctional, all used for different purposes at other times. The sacredness is now not in the place but in the presence of Christ among his people according to his Word. The meeting place can be a home, a catacomb, an open-air amphitheatre. Why then should we not also use the space where we worship together as the people of God, for lunches, youth group activities and various evangelistic initiatives?

We twenty-first-century Christians need to challenge ourselves as to the message we communicate by our attitude to our buildings. The gospel says, 'Go!', but our buildings tend to say, 'Stay where you are!' The gospel says, 'Seek the lost!', but the message of our church buildings is often 'Let the lost seek the church!'[37] Could it be that buildings that should subserve our gospel endeavours, can sometimes actually hinder them?

This is just one example of where entrenched attitudes need to be disturbed by accurate biblical exegesis and practice in order for us to be freed up to use all our facilities with the aim that people may be reached with the life-giving message of the gospel.

If we are honest, many of us would have to admit that behind our entrenched attitudes is often a fear of what other people will say or think. Any change demanded by convictions freshly hammered out on the anvil of biblical exegesis will engender criticism. It is all too easy for the over-sensitive or ill-informed consciences of others to capture ours. Those in the background of our lives, in church and family networks, can become the main influencers of our thinking and practice. (Sometimes they seem to be in the foreground!) We need to get a wise understanding of what is going on here and develop the right priority: 'We must obey God rather than men' (Acts 5:29). Other people's opinions, however much we respect those people, must always be tested by the Word of God. The Bible itself reminds us how flimsy is reliance on mere humans. It is not for nothing that the prophet Isaiah tells us to 'Stop regarding man in whose nostrils is breath, for of what account is he' (Is. 2:22). The fact that we human beings breathe through our nostrils is a vivid reminder of our fragility (our breath will soon cease) and of the folly of giving too much weight to human opinions. The path of true wisdom is well expressed by

37 Stuart Murray, *Church Planting* (Carlisle: Paternoster, 1998) p. 209.

the proverb, 'The fear of man lays a snare, but whoever trusts the LORD is safe' (Prov. 29:25).

Style of leadership

One of the difficulties with the historic 'pastor and deacons' ministry model is that it can lead to over-dependence on one man. It is too easy for an authoritarian, dictatorial style of leadership to develop. Change can happen under this model. It can even happen more easily than under a more consultative style of leadership. It can even appear to be gospel-driven change, but people are cowed and browbeaten into it. The biblical model of plural eldership safeguards against this.

Leadership and authority in New Testament terms is never about status or hierarchy. As soon as we begin to talk about 'office' in the church the danger is that we revert to worldly stereotypes. Our default is to think in terms of position and power.

Make no mistake, New Testament elders are required to rule. They are exhorted to rule well (1 Tim. 5:17), and New Testament Christians are exhorted to honour them, remember them, obey them and submit to them (1 Tim. 5:17; Heb. 13:7, 17). There is real God-given authority in the church of Jesus Christ. But the *model* is service not status. Our great leader, Jesus Christ himself, said:

> You know that those who are considered rulers of the Gentiles lord it over them, and their great ones exercise authority over them. But it shall not be so among you. But whoever would be

great among you must be your servant, and whoever would be first
among you must be slave of all. For even the Son of Man came not
to be served but to serve, and to give his life as a ransom for many
(Mk. 10:42-45).

The biblical model of rule is humble service. In a good restaurant,
it is all about those who sit at the table. They are the ones being
served. The waiters are simply serving them, considering their
needs, taking away from them duties that would be onerous
and unwelcome. By ruling well, elders of churches serve the
people. They take away from them the arduous responsibility
– and it is arduous – of ruling. Church members can come to
church meetings, for example, knowing that they are released
from the burden of ruling the church. This should bring great
relief and, with it, an understanding of limitation of role. While
church members appoint the elders, and even dismiss them
for false teaching,[38] it is not their role or responsibility before
God to put their leaders right on every point or to set the
direction of the church. The New Testament pattern is not a
democracy swayed by a majority or indeed held hostage by
an intransigent minority. Many churches have come to grief
trying to follow a secular model for church government.

Church leaders are accountable to God and to each other
for their leadership. Whatever the issue, they must study the
Word and submit to it, pray, and engage in gracious discussion
among themselves. There must be a willingness to practice

---

38 See Mike Gilbart-Smith's chapter on 'Independency' in David Skull,
Andrew King and Jim Sayers (eds), *Pure Church* (London: Grace
Publications, 2018).

mutual submission (1 Pet. 5:5). This may include a minority view being willing to submit to the majority, but it always involves seeking to discern and do the will of the Lord Jesus, never seeking to pursue a personal agenda. Thus the New Testament pattern of plural eldership provides wise checks and balances.

Elders do not discuss the affairs of the church, or lead them, in any detached kind of way. These men are *shepherds*. They are supposed to know their sheep. They must be sensitive to, and willing to reflect back in elders' meetings, the range of views and personalities there are in the church. All this means that discussions at eldership level can be stressful. Concern over issues can lead to a sleepless night. Spiritual maturity is required and relationships within the eldership closely protected. Yet it is the Lord's provision for his church that its elders, and not the body of the church, should take the heavy end of the burden of stress.

It may be that in a group of elders one man, perhaps the only paid pastor, is first among equals. Nonetheless, the basic model is of team ministry.

> So I exhort the elders among you, as a fellow elder and a witness of the sufferings of Christ, as well as a partaker of the glory that is to be revealed: shepherd the flock of God that is among you, exercising oversight, not under compulsion, but willingly, as God would have you; not for shameful gain, but eagerly; not domineering over those in your charge, but being examples to the flock. And when the chief Shepherd appears, you will receive the unfading crown of glory (1 Pet. 5:1-4).

When I began my ministry at Rehoboth one of the deacons wisely said to me, 'You can only lead people as far as they will follow.' I have never forgotten this. In managing gospel-driven change, under-shepherds must carry their people with them. We must respect our people and listen to them. It requires gentle, firm, pastoral, visionary leadership.

Nevertheless, the key thing about being a shepherd is not rule but care for the flock. A true shepherd loves his sheep and will not abandon them. He has strong protective instincts towards them. When they suffer, he suffers with them; when they rejoice, he is glad. He desires that they should be well fed. If the leadership in a church is not *loving*, something has gone seriously wrong. The standard is high. Often over the years we have asked with the apostle Paul, 'who is sufficient for these things?' (2 Cor. 2:16). We have the same answer he did, 'our sufficiency is from God' (2 Cor. 3:5).

Peaceful church meetings

Where a church has a formal membership, its decision-making is usually discussed and ratified in a meeting of members. This is variously called the members' meeting or the business meeting, the annual general meeting or in some contexts the annual parochial church meeting. Nomenclature is not inconsequential. These descriptions can too easily evoke a secular model. It is strange how otherwise godly people can change their spirit and behaviour when they come to what they understand to be the business meeting. Suddenly they are back in the committee room or on the shop floor, in the union or board meeting. Their approach becomes adversarial. They speak and behave in a way they would not dream of doing in a worship service of the church.

For this reason, I am convinced that such meetings should aim to be as spiritual as any other meeting of the church. Why not pray your way through the meeting? Why not have times of prayer before and after major decisions? Why not pray for conversions, for revival, for cases of pastoral need in these meetings? Open the Bible. Sing the praises of King Jesus. Do all you can to foster fellowship. The church is coming together as the body of Christ to seek the will of Christ. This awareness should be in the heart and mind of every member. In such a context people who make hasty, critical or opinionated comments should be gently but firmly rebuked.

People who have come to HCC from other churches, often having been hurt or damaged by their experience of church life, have commented on the peaceful and pleasant nature of our church meetings. This has been hard won and cannot be taken for granted. I have referred to a period in our church life, in the 1970s, where there was a lot of church trouble with some difficult church meetings, full of strife. On occasions you felt you could cut the atmosphere with a knife. Everyone found those meetings stressful. As the apostle James says in a similar context, 'My brothers, these things ought not to be so' (Jas. 3:10).

Our present approach to church meetings has come as a direct result of our prayer and determination that, by the grace of God, the church should never again suffer in this way. We want to be able to treasure and enjoy peaceful church meetings. We want jealously to guard our spirits and attitudes as we approach them. In fact, we have now made this a teaching point and have produced a document for all members with the title *Peaceful Church Meetings*. Let me give you a flavour of it.

The introduction refers to our past experience of church conflict and has this paragraph:

> ... as the church grows, and we sometimes face difficult and challenging issues for decision, there is potential danger that we forget what it takes to maintain peace, and we lose our present blessings.

There is then reference to a section on *The Local Church and Church Life* in our members' handbook where there are paragraphs on the government of the church, meetings of the church and the importance of loyalty and unity. The big picture is that the church belongs to Jesus and is directly accountable to him. 'In doing his will, our individual opinions, and what each of us thinks or prefers is utterly secondary.'

In referring to the role of elders it states that many church decisions involve applying Bible principles in which a variety of decisions would be possible. A unanimous recommendation from the elders then carries considerable weight. On big and difficult decisions, elders sometimes take a long time to come to the position where they can make a unanimous recommendation to the church:

> Elders are servant leaders. We believe it is right to consult church

members on big decisions. We will always listen very carefully to what you tell us because we are acutely aware of our weakness, and that the Lord may speak to us through you. If the final outcome of a consultation told us that opinion in the church was significantly divided ... or there was a sense of confusion, then we would defer bringing it forward for decision to allow more time for reflection and prayer.

In this document, the elders then address the relative responsibilities of church members as follows:

We greatly value the way you pray for us and the church. Please continue to do that. Please keep a sense of perspective. There are lots of comparatively small decisions where we must be willing to accept an outcome we wouldn't prefer. Please take the effort to respond when we consult you, or ask for feedback ... We want to emphasise that if you do have concerns about something we are consulting on (or anything else) then please tell us. We are always willing to visit you so as to fully understand your thoughts. If you have questions or concerns please never wait until a church meeting to express them. Tell us as soon as possible so that we can pray, consider and respond to you. It is possible that even after all the above, there may be an elders' recommendation with which you definitely disagree, and you feel you must express that disagreement. At the church meeting you have the option of either abstaining or voting against. In either case, if the recommendation is carried, then it is essential that you graciously submit to the decision. You can do this with peace since you have discharged your responsibility before God as a member of his church. Also we must, of course, all continue to love each other. Because it is the elders' responsibility to lead the church, and because a unanimous recommendation from the elders must carry considerable weight, then if you are unsure how to vote, you should support the elders' recommendation.

This principle of discharging your conscience before God is, I believe, of crucial importance in church life. By it, you clearly communicate what conscientiously you believe, by word, by vote or both. When it is done, it is done. Unless it is a matter of fundamental gospel truth, you can then safely leave it with God and submit lovingly, even joyfully, to your brothers and sisters in Christ. This is surely what the apostle Paul means when he writes of unity as an endeavour:

> I therefore, a prisoner for the Lord, urge you to walk in a manner worthy of the calling to which you have been called, with all humility and gentleness, with patience, bearing with one another in love, eager to maintain the unity of the Spirit in the bond of peace (Eph. 4:1-3).

To maintain the unity of the Spirit is a matter of strenuous effort. In a sermon on this text in Ephesians, John Bunyan says:

> How needful ... is it for Christians to distinguish, if ever they would be at peace and unity, between those truths which are essential to church-communion, and those that are not! ... Brethren, did we all agree that we were erring in many things, we should soon agree to go to God, and pray for more wisdom and revelation of his mind and will concerning us. But here is our misery, that we no sooner receive anything for truth, but we presently ascend the chair of

infallibility with it, as though in this we could not err ...[39]

He enunciates the principle that on secondary matters, where godly people have often differed, we should agree to disagree agreeably. Our paper on 'Peaceful Church Meetings' concludes like this:

> The devil hates all true Christian churches. He does his best to sow discord and division because he knows it grieves the Holy Spirit and ruins a church's usefulness and witness. Each one of us is a potential entry point for the enemy. Hopefully this note will enable us all to resist him.

It is a sobering thought that I could be the entry point, the agent used, by the enemy of souls to do a wrecking work in the church of Jesus Christ. 'Uphold my steps in your paths that my footsteps may not slip' (Ps. 17:5, NKJV).

Properly agreed change in church life, then, is change brought for the sake of the gospel by the church's leadership. It is not what the pastor wants, or what the deacon with the strongest personality wants. It is not what the older people want or what the young people want. It is not even what the majority wants. It is what godly people have given time and thought and prayer to, in careful consultation with others, to try to discern what the Lord Jesus wants. We must never forget that this is his church bought by his precious blood (Acts 20:28). She must be guided by the biblical principle of the mutual submission of her members to one another out of

---

39 John Bunyan, 'An exhortation to Peace and Unity', *The Works of John Bunyan*, Vol. 2 (Blackie and Son, 1688), pp. 743–754.

reverence for Christ (Eph. 5:21). Psalm 133 presents a beautiful portrait of unity and shows that such oneness is the place where God 'commands the blessing' (Ps. 133:3, my emphasis). Change is always a potential threat to unity, because people find change difficult. Disunity is a poor witness. Therefore, to manage change well is of the utmost importance in church life.

The biblical principle of selflessness

Closely connected with all of this is the Bible teaching about self-denial. Resistance to right, gospel-driven change often comes because of selfishness. People put personal preference above the needs of others. When we changed our hymnbook, for example, we asked our folk to consider the needs of the present and future congregation, not their own personal preferences. It helped people stand outside their own skin and see things slightly differently. My personal preference is often for the old hymns; to embrace more modern styles and compositions is in some ways for me a sacrifice. However, if we are not compromising biblical truth but bringing it to people in a way that is more accessible to them then should we not do it *for their sake*?

Again, the way in which change is managed is of crucial importance. There are ways of holding on to what is best in the old at the same time as embracing what is best in the new. For ourselves at HCC, on this issue of singing the praises of God, we have recognised two genres both in lyrics and in music. The traditional music for the older hymns is four-part harmony accompanied by piano or organ, or both.

Many contemporary worship songs are of a different genre and are more effectively accompanied by guitar and other instruments. The way we currently express this at HCC is by singing the more traditional hymns with organ and piano, and more contemporary hymns with a small music group with piano. The emphasis is on worship, not performance, and the essential criterion is the biblical content, power and accuracy of what is sung. All must be done reverently and joyfully, to the best of our ability and to the glory of God.

This is just one area in which selflessness needs to be practised. It is interesting that the New Testament passages dealing with our sung praise emphasise its impact on 'one another':

> ... addressing *one another* in psalms and hymns and spiritual songs, singing and making melody to the Lord with your heart, giving thanks always and for everything to God the Father in the name of our Lord Jesus Christ, submitting to *one another* out of reverence for Christ (Eph. 5:19-21, my emphasis).

This pathway of mutual submission and selflessness brings us close to Jesus who teaches so vividly the crucifixion of the self - particularly applicable to matters of personal preference in church life. Where the Bible allows genuine freedom, very often our own preference is in the forefront of our minds. This 'wanting my way' is a burden we should be willing to lay at the foot of the cross. What is best for others? What is good for communicating the gospel, or helping the worship of others, within biblical parameters? These are truly gospel-hearted questions, and, when answered with a willingness to submit to one another and to the leadership of a church, will bear the hallmark of the 'Spirit of Christ' (Rom. 8:9; 1 Pet. 1:11).

Sensitivity to the views and needs of others should be balanced, however, by a willingness to act courageously according to biblical conviction. A refusal to do a right thing because of what other people might say or think is just another form of self-centredness. The love of self craves ease and the good opinion of others. Gospel obedience is bound to take us on the path of crucifixion of the self.

The biblical principle of intelligibility

I have wrestled with this throughout my ministry, and definitely need the help of others to think it through and apply it consistently. The bottom line is that I have come to believe it to be a biblical principle. The Word of God must be delivered in language that is understood. Our worship needs to be accessible in its forms of language to those who participate. It is not simply a matter of 'thees' and 'thous' but also of 'lays' and 'lauds'.[40] The apostle Paul says:

> If even lifeless instruments, such as the flute or the harp, do not give distinct notes, how will anyone know what is played? And if the bugle gives an indistinct sound, who will get ready for battle? So with yourselves, if with your tongue you utter speech that is not intelligible, how will anyone know what is said? For you will be

---

40 'Lay' and 'laud' are both praise words that appear in our hymnody, such as 'Awake, my soul, in joyful lays' or 'All glory, laud and honour'.

speaking into the air ... in church I would rather speak five words with my mind in order to instruct others, than ten thousand words in a tongue (1 Cor. 14:7-9,19).

He is dealing with the issue of speaking in tongues, but the principle of intelligibility undergirds the teaching.

The famous pulpit passage in the book of Nehemiah is also highly relevant, where there is a strong emphasis on the understanding. We are told that 'the ears of all the people were attentive to the Book of the Law', and that the leaders 'helped the people to understand the Law ... They read from the book, from the Law of God, clearly, and they gave the meaning, so that the people understood the reading' (Neh. 8:3-8).

The importance of intelligibility began to come home to me early in my ministry when I read these words of J.C. Ryle, the great Anglican evangelical bishop:

> I felt that I was doing the country people in my congregation [of Exbury] no good whatever. I was shooting over their heads; they could not understand my imitation of Melville's style, which I thought much of, therefore I thought it my plain duty to crucify my style and bring it down to what it is now.[41]

The people in our congregation in Coventry are not country people but ethnically and socially mixed city dwellers. I am a middle-class country boy with an instinctive, inherited theological vocabulary and attendant phraseology. If J.C. Ryle made deliberate, strenuous and manly efforts to speak to

41 Eric Russell, J.C. Ryle: That Man of Granite with the Heart of a Child (Tain: Christian Focus Publications), p. 60.

the 'plain man' in his day, then so should I in mine. He was ministering in an age of oratorical flourish, but it is striking that his writings are still far more accessible to the twenty-first-century reader than those of most of his Victorian contemporaries. His written style undoubtedly reflects his spoken word.

Picking this up, J.I. Packer describes J.C. Ryle's:

> brisk, spare, punchy style ... its cultivated forcefulness, its use of the simplest words, its fusillades of short, one-clause sentences ... its rib-jabbing drumbeat rhetoric, its easy logical flow, its total lack of sentimentality, and its resolve to call a spade a spade.[42]

I have referred to my studies, mid-pastorate, at the Evangelical Theological College of Wales. This was an opportunity to pause and reflect on my ministry, and discuss issues with other pastors in a collegiate way. One of the assignments was to submit a couple of sermons to the course director for his comments and feedback. This was daunting: but one of the most useful exercises I have ever undertaken. The comments were kind, but one particular observation stood out. He pointed out that I was speaking in rather long sentences: perhaps in a more literary style than was good for direct, effective communication. This gave momentum to me in doing my own version of Ryle's 'crucifixion' of speaking style. When I first started to preach, I used a very extemporary style drawing on the phraseology that came naturally to me. If ever

---

42 J.I. Packer, *Faithfulness and Holiness* (Wheaton: Crossway, 2010), p. 19.

I find the courage to listen to my early attempts at preaching – usually on tape – I am distinctly embarrassed!

In this connection, I still remember my shock when I first read Dr Martyn Lloyd-Jones's *Preaching and Preachers* and discovered his recommendation that preachers write out in full at least one sermon every week. Coming from a background that did not even permit notes in the pulpit, this seemed like heresy. Was it not quenching the Spirit? Yet as the years have gone by, I have realised increasingly that preachers must think and prepare carefully not only what we are going to say, but how we are going to say it: and on some occasions, the precise words we will use. As we do this, we need to visualise the very people, and kinds of people, to whom we expect to be speaking. We must sit where they sit, imagine what it is like to be them, as we bring to them the Word of God, and the startling message of free salvation and sins forgiven.

James Young has been instrumental in our church in helping us think through and apply the issue of intelligibility in a more thoroughgoing way. This has not been without pain. I think of breakfast meetings in a café in Hillfields Square in the early years of James' involvement in the work, in which we wrestled with issues around being contemporary and accessible, especially in the language and genre of our sung praise. There were at times significant differences of perspective. In the process of listening to one another, respecting one another, at times agreeing to disagree, we found a way forward, proving the proverb true, 'iron sharpens iron, and one man sharpens another' (Prov. 27:17). It is doubtful that real progress is likely to be made in such areas without a certain amount of gracious friction. Those of us with a more conservative mind-set and perspective would scarcely move very far without it. Differences of detail, and preference, will of course persist, but where there is a shared aim, and the biblical principle agreed, with give and take, there is always a God-honouring way through.

This intelligibility principle is of particular importance in a setting where some people are struggling to learn English, others have special needs, and not all are highly educated or use middle-class forms of speech. We aim therefore in the spoken word not to assume knowledge of the Bible or of church history and its famous characters. If we quote Spurgeon or Calvin, for example, we explain to people who they are. As a policy, we avoid all Elizabethan language in our worship, both spoken and sung, except where there are issues of copyright. We need to think carefully about our vocabulary and how accessible it is to all parts of the congregation. This principle is not rocket science, but, as we work at it, it's bound to challenge us. When I first started to preach, my then pastor said to me, 'aim at the twelve-year-olds'. I guess what we have been doing is trying to follow through on that advice. It is all about loving the people.

It is not therefore the case, as some would have it, that all attempts to be contemporary and accessible in our language and style of worship are, by definition, a sign of theological compromise or downgrade. It is a worthy and biblical endeavour to remove unnecessary obstacles from people's comprehension and reception of the gospel message.

The biblical principle of 'one another'

An unwholesome development, especially in the history of the western church, is an over-emphasis on our individual preferences, needs and opinions. Of course, we come to Christ as individuals. Of the church as Zion, God's people, it is said 'this one and that one were born in her' (Ps. 87:5, NKJV). We are baptised and join the church as individuals. Our Christian testimony is personal. We have individual gifts. Is there a danger, however, that we then assess churches on how well they cater for the individual? The result is that church attendance becomes a consumer product. The New Testament model is much more organic and communal. When we join a local assembly of believers, we join a body, a family, a community. We function within that body as individual members of the whole.

It is striking how many references there are in the New Testament to the way believers are to relate to one another. The springboard is the new commandment of Jesus:

> A new commandment I give to you, that you love one another: just as I have loved you, you also are to love one another. By this all people will know that you are my disciples, if you have love for one another (Jn. 13:34–35).

Here we have two new things: a new model, Jesus' own humble self-giving love ('love one another as I have loved you'), and the emergence of a new community, the church, in which disciples are commanded to love another. It is a vital aspect of the testimony of the church to a watching world. The foot washing of John 13 demonstrates humble, selfless service. The love that Jesus modelled is a persistent, dogged love: an unworldly love that will not let go or give up. When things go wrong in relationships in the world the default is to distance yourself or ultimately ditch the relationship – find another friend, or another marriage partner. In the church of Jesus, however, things should be different, especially at the point when things go wrong or relationships become strained. Too often the Christian default has become to go shopping for another church.

The apostle John never forgot what he saw and heard from Jesus in the upper room. His letters at the end of the New Testament represent about two per cent of the New Testament, but twenty per cent of the number of times the word 'love' occurs. Because God loved us, we ought to love one another. How else can the love of God be demonstrated unless among the actual brothers and sisters that we see and know?

The New Testament teaching is that Christians are one body in Christ and individually members of one another. Therefore we should not judge one another, we should never go to court against one another, never be vicious or unkind, or provoke or envy or lie to one another. We should never speak evil about or grumble against one another. Rather we are to increase and abound in love to one another, to have fervent love between us; to be kindly affectionate, likeminded, to give preference to one another, admonish one another, care for, serve, bear with and forgive one another. In our worship we are to speak to one another in psalms and hymns and spiritual songs. We are to submit to one another, pray for one another, have compassion for one another, be hospitable to one another. We should always greet one another warmly.[43]

Provocation can indeed take place, but it must only be to love and good works. The fellowship and communal life of Christians is vital. We must not forsake the assembling of ourselves together (Heb. 10:24–25). We must always encourage each other.

Real Christian love is thus incarnational in the family of the people of God. It has shape and dimensions. There is behaviour that conforms to it and behaviour that does not. Authentic Christianity should always be visible in the conduct and attitude of its followers.

The early church, as depicted in the Acts of the Apostles, is very evidently a community of a shared love and a shared life.[44] When we lay this alongside our present experience of church life, it is a vision that calls for radical change in attitudes, in behaviour, and indeed in organisation and activity.

The biblical principle of Jesus-centredness

The key to all the principles involved in managing gospel-

---

43 Bible references in order summarised: Rom. 12:5; Eph. 4:25; Rom. 14:13; 1 Cor. 6:1,7; 1 Pet. 2:1; 1 Cor. 13:4; Jas. 4:11; Jas. 5:9; 1 Thess. 3:12; 1 Pet. 4:8; Rom. 12:10; Rom. 15:5; Rom. 15:14; 1 Cor. 12:25; Gal. 5:13; 1 Pet. 4:10; Rom. 15:1; Col. 3:13; Eph. 4:32; 1 Pet. 5:5; Jas. 5:16; 1 Pet. 4:9; Rom. 16:16.

44 See for example Acts 2:42-47; Acts 4:32-37; Acts 6:1-7.

driven change must surely be the centrality of the person and work of Jesus Christ. The early Christian church was wonderfully Christ-centred. Its great concern was that in all things he should be pre-eminent (Col. 1:18).

It has to be admitted that our resistance to good and right change in church life is often the result of self-centredness. The apostle Paul defines Christians as 'those who live no longer to themselves' (2 Cor. 5:15). This is breathtakingly new. Its secret is not duty or obligation or asceticism. Its frame of reference is not what other people are saying or thinking. Its concern is not our name or reputation or standing in Christian circles. Rather it is a constraint, a compulsion – 'for the love of Christ controls us' (2 Cor. 5:14).

When a whole company of believers is motivated and controlled by the love of Jesus, who for our sake died and rose again, it stands to reason that it will be distinguishable, set apart, for that very thing. It will be a community that is ever moving onwards and upwards, reformed and reforming. It would not be at all surprising if its radical values and lifestyle expose it to the persecution of the world. It would be sad, but again not surprising, if some of the opposition comes from those who are resistant to gospel-driven change within its own ranks.

Chapter 8
Some Practicalities

Because of our inherent resistance to change, together with a natural, and commendable, reluctance to 'rock the boat', we need to be both creative and strategic about maintaining the momentum of gospel-driven change in church life. The major responsibility for this lies with a church's leadership. Here are a few policies and practices which undoubtedly help in this process.

Communication, communication, communication

Clear, upfront, well-timed communication is vital to navigating gospel-driven change. When a change is envisaged in church life, it is often the subject of protracted discussions in elders' meetings, taking place sometimes over months, even years. When the way forward is agreed, it is a great mistake then to try to hurry it through a meeting of the members. It is just not fair to spring significant change on people in a single meeting, or to expect them to cast their vote, if it is a voting matter, there and then. The elders have become familiar with the issues. The body of the church now needs time to pray, ask questions, consider.

This reflects the reality that, in addition to the responsibility of elders to rule, the New Testament pattern for church life is also consultative. The role of the whole gathering is not simply to rubber stamp what the elders have decided. Where a church has a membership, the prayerful, joyful endorsement of the membership is an essential part of the process. When the first deacons were appointed, we are told that what the apostles said 'pleased the whole gathering, and they chose ...' (Acts 6:5). It was the whole gathering who chose the men.

The device of informing church members of proposed major change by letter (or email) prior to a meeting has distinct benefits. It enables a proper setting out of the issues. It can indicate the spirit and tone of the discussions among the elders. It can include the biblical reasoning behind the proposed change. It gives the opportunity to anticipate and clarify possible misunderstandings. It can give detail that is sometimes difficult to absorb in a meeting. It can invite questions, comments and feedback before the meeting. Elders have the opportunity to visit people who may be struggling with what is proposed, so that, when it comes to the meeting itself, they are informed and prepared. Even with this method, it is often wise in one meeting to give notice of a vote that will take place in the next. People do need time to absorb and adjust, to think and to pray.

A questionnaire to church members can also be a helpful part of the process in moving forward major issues. Again, it gives people space and opportunity to indicate what they really think. The members' responses can then be considered and taken into account in the way change is managed, and in the pastoral care of people during it.

Whatever the method, the principal thing in managing gospel-driven change is effective communication. To try to rush things through, or bring them in via the back door, is a recipe for disaster. It is vital to be sensitive to the kind of impact proposed change is likely to have on people.

Timing

It follows that patience is required. There is not only a right thing to do, but a right time to do it, as in the wisdom book, Ecclesiastes, 'For there is a time and a way for everything' (Ecc. 8:6). Many a young or new pastor has been in too much of a hurry, and brought division and confusion into the life of the church.

It took us years at HCC to change our Bible version and work through issues connected with the role of women; years for us to be led to the right use of a legacy. No doubt change can happen too slowly, due to a kind of paralysis setting in caused by fear or indecision, but I think more damage is done by trying to force the pace. In church life, as in our personal walk with God, we need to pray our way along. We do not know what lies ahead. Ultimately, there is a simplicity about it all – the will, and the timing, of the great Head of the Church is the only thing that matters.

Trial periods

Reference has already been made to the first time we used a trial period to test and assess a proposed major change. The issue was the participation of women in the public prayer life of the church. We had come to a point of impasse: then one of the men who had been opposed to the proposed change suggested that we implement it for a trial period.

Coming from the source it did, it was a significant concession. It had the advantage of bringing transparency to the whole church about the debate that had taken place at leadership level. We emphasised that it was a genuine trial and not a way of bringing change in by default. During this time, we would be especially sensitive to watch for the Lord's guidance. We agreed that we could all pray that if the change was not in the Lord's will for his church, that he would make it clear to us during the trial period. That could be by giving us a clearer light on Scripture. It could be by withdrawing the spirit of prayer that we had in the church. It could be by encouraging us in our church prayer life.

In this specific case, the trial period confirmed the practice and helped some of those who questioned it. It did not result, as some had feared, in anyone pushing themselves forward conspicuously in prayer, but rather in a deepened communal prayer life. Since then, we have used a trial period more than once in managing change. It has to be borne in mind, of course, that it is a method that does inevitably give momentum to a proposed change: and one that is always capable of evoking a somewhat cynical response: 'trial periods always lead to adoption'. Nonetheless, if done conscientiously, the option of drawing back from the change is a real one.

A helpful practice – feedback

In this connection, we have found it helpful to foster an expectation of feedback in all our ministries. It is now understood that after preaching, or leading, or doing a Bible reading or talk – after involvement in any ministry at all – any one of us may receive constructive written feedback, usually from one of the elders. It is important that this happens right across the board, and that all the elders are able to give such feedback to each other. Not even the senior pastor or lead elder is exempt. The fact that it becomes a regular feature of church life rescues it from it happening only when people get things badly wrong.

Feedback must always be constructive. There are always things to be positive and appreciative about. Suggestions for improvement can be put tactfully in a section on 'things to think about'. In this way unhelpful habits can be corrected, or incorrect exposition challenged.

Regular, prayerful elders' meetings

Eldership, as has already been illustrated, is both an onerous and a collective responsibility. Elders' meetings need to take place with sufficient regularity to ensure not only the supervision of the week-by-week life of the church and its 'bread and butter' pastoral issues, but also the discussion of long-term goals and vision. This needs plenty of space and must not be rushed or squeezed out. In particular, it is vital to make time for praying together. It is disastrous if elders' meetings become simply about getting through an agenda motivated by a kind of business mentality. These are spiritual meetings of spiritually-minded men, and it is just not adequate for them simply to begin and end with a kind of statutory, formal prayer. Here is a group of people who really need to grow in their fellowship in prayer. It is so often as we pray that we begin to discern the Lord's will. When together we wrestle for wisdom, for guidance and for unity, we are much less likely to want to drive a personal agenda or adopt an adversarial, issues-based approach to the life of the church.

Retreats

The regular meetings of the elders, or church leadership, can wisely be supplemented by occasional whole day retreats. The opportunity to get away from our normal surroundings and to spend quality time on one or two big issues can be very refreshing and productive. When we have done this at HCC, we have often spent the first hour or so sharing our own personal and family situations and praying for each other – in itself a uniting experience. To be able to share a meal, go for a walk, laugh together, as well as to discuss our long-term vision, is beneficial. Busy elders' meetings can often develop a backlog of matters to consider, and a well-timed retreat can be very helpful in moving things forward. Where there are differences of opinion within the leadership, plenty of time needs to be given for reflective listening. It is good practice to be able to reflect back to one another what we thought we heard each other say. It can bring much greater clarity to a discussion and avoid misunderstandings.

Sabbaticals

Working from the same principles, it can also be enormously beneficial for full-time workers to be able to enjoy a sabbatical. These were not part of the long tradition of the church at HCC, and indeed I had been a pastor for twenty-one years before I took my first sabbatical. If you adopt the policy of one every seven years, by then I was due three!

However regularly it is done, or how it is managed, will vary in different situations. The stated purpose of a sabbatical will also depend on circumstances. Where there is exhaustion or burnout, its purpose will largely be rest and recovery. Where there are heavy preaching responsibilities, the aim might be to read and study without having the pressure of needing to prepare a sermon or two for next Sunday. It can be so helpful to give attention perhaps to a neglected part of Scripture. In a regular preaching ministry, there can be a sense of water flowing 'straight in and straight out'. The opportunity to develop a little reservoir is most beneficial. Another major purpose of a sabbatical may be to reflect on current trends in church life and to network with, and visit, other churches, pastors and ministries. Whatever its stated purpose, a sabbatical gives the opportunity to restore perspective and get a bird's eye view of the work to which we are called.

Fraternals

However supportive a church may be to its leadership, and however strong the team spirit of its leadership, those in full time ministry often find it to be a lonely pathway. Who is going to pastor the pastors? Often this need can be met by a healthy association life. Many churches fiercely guard the autonomy of the local church, but this needs to be tempered by the mutual accountability and fellowship of inter-dependence. Local fraternals and national (even international) church partnerships can be fruitful in providing advice, support and fellowship. When a pastor is struggling to navigate change at home it can be so helpful to talk and pray with others who have faced similar issues. Networking with others can keep us from going out on a limb or from developing unrealistic expectations.

The issue of succession

My relationship with HCC as a pastor has never had a professional feel about it. I was never called for an interview, or a face-to-face with church members before I was appointed. They already knew me. I was, since first arriving as a student in 1969, home-grown. By the time I was appointed pastor I had already been serving as a deacon in the church for some years, and from within it a gift of preaching had been recognised.

It seems good to me, and in line with New Testament teaching, when the gifts needed to lead a church are found within it. The apostle Paul left Titus in Crete so that he might appoint elders in every town. These must have come from within those churches (Titus 1:5; see also Acts 14:23). It also seems good when there can be smooth and natural transitions between ministries. It happened at the beginning of my ministry as a pastor, and by the grace of God, it is happening at the end.

There is actually nothing in the Bible, so far as I can see, directly about retirement. Preaching the gospel is a calling. It is surely right for a man with this vocation to serve God, with the health and strength he gives, to the best of his ability and for the rest of his days. Yet there is also a right time to recognise that the onerous responsibilities associated with being a pastor or senior pastor must, because of age and declining faculties, be relinquished. This can happen at a different age for different men.

In the Strict Baptist circles from which I come, pastors do not usually retire. My grandfather, who was a pastor for over forty years at Linslade in Bedfordshire, died in harness at the age of eighty-four. About two weeks before he died he preached his final sermons, knowing they were his last, on 'I have fought the good fight ...' (2 Tim. 4:7). There is something deeply attractive about that and in a smaller church it can be sustainable.

It can also be problematic. It is possible for men to stay on in a position, to a large extent unaware that their faculties and grasp on things are failing. When they die, they can leave a church in a weakened state, unprepared for succession, the church having been too dependent on one man. In a larger church the heavy demands and responsibilities of a busy scene and diverse community mean that retirement is not only wise but essential. Wisdom dictates that it should be properly anticipated and prepared for, not delayed.

It has also become conventional wisdom to advise that retiring pastors should move right away from their church in order to make room for the next man. It can be deeply unhelpful if the people are always looking over their shoulder at the previous incumbent, or if the man himself cannot help trying to influence the direction of the church from the side-lines. It is not easy for a new pastor to have the old one in his congregation, though there have been examples, depending on the character and spirit of both men, where this has very happily been the case. It is perhaps wise to say that in most cases the best policy is for a retired pastor to leave the church where he has served.

Yet think again. The New Testament pattern of church life is one where the church is a spiritual family, a new community of God's grace, where people are bound together in mutual love, support and covenant relationship. Should such a community be over-influenced by a secular and prudential model of retirement? There must surely be a godly way forward.

For Hazel and me what is now Hillfields Church Coventry has been our spiritual home for fifty years. We have known what it is to be in the church without being in office. Our roots in the church go very deep. Our dearest friends, and some of our family, are there. Are we really saying that this church in which we have served all our adult lives should not also be our church as we come to the evening of our lives?

We feel that we have been blessed by the gracious hand of God on the situation as we have prepared for succession. The key has been the development, over time, of a team approach to leadership and ministry. In particular the fact that James and I have worked alongside each other for twenty years, men of contrasting personalities in developing roles, has meant that neither is a threat to the other. We have sought not to major on status or position. We have not used the language of ownership. This has undoubtedly helped with transition. Even so, I realise that I need still to be vigilant and proactive in weaning people off any tendency to think that I am the guardian of the old school within the church.

I first began to give notice to the church of the need to anticipate and prepare for transition shortly after my sixtieth birthday. It was in that same year, providentially, that we appointed James, already serving as an elder in the church, as a co-pastor. At that stage I indicated that I thought the age sixty-five was a likely benchmark for my retirement. Various health issues strengthened the case. In point of fact, having another pastor alongside meant that I was able to share preaching and other pastoral responsibilities and thus to continue as a pastor for longer than anticipated.

The transition that has now taken place has been gradual, almost seamless. With a growing church, I was realising increasingly that I must hand over the overall burden of responsibility for the work that I had carried for over thirty years. The outcome of this was that in 2016, in my sixty-sixth year, we appointed James as the lead elder. This meant that I stepped down from being the senior pastor, taking a commensurate drop in salary. James did not feel he could fulfil precisely the same role in the church I had done, but was willing to take on that ultimate kind of spiritual and administrative responsibility which is a reality for a senior pastor. This meant that I could continue my preaching and pastoral work in the church but in a reduced capacity and with a lesser role. I continued as an elder.

During the next couple of years we began looking for another man to work with us either as a trainee minister or a co-pastor. I was finding the demands of preaching twice in succession on a Sunday morning increasingly tiring. We needed a younger man to help us. This resulted in the appointment in May 2019 of Simon Hook as a co-pastor. Si is an experienced preacher/pastor and a wonderful addition to the team.

The latest development has now been for me, at age seventy, to retire fully from being a paid pastor. I have been able to do this in the knowledge that, by God's grace, faithful, gospel-hearted men are in place, willing and able to feed and lead the church. It was the unanimous view of the current eldership that I should continue for the time being to serve the church as a low-profile elder. This would not be possible apart from the development of a team approach to ministry in which a changing situation can be accommodated and publicly recognised.

In addition to the two full-time pastors, we also currently have four other paid church workers, working in ministry and administrative roles, either in a full-time or part-time capacity.

Chapter 9
Slippery slopes and bath water

Any attempt to apply non-biblical proverbial wisdom to the church of Jesus Christ must be handled with care. Yet most of us will have heard the concept of 'the slippery slope' applied rather carelessly to change in church life. Change is often resisted, or delayed, because people are afraid of this slippery slope. They wonder where it is all leading.

However, our concept of *gospel*-driven change *ought* to mean that such fears are not well-grounded. At the point where proposed change becomes weak in biblical rationale, it must be resisted strenuously. One of the skills in skiing is knowing when and how to stop! With skill it can be done.

There are, however, warnings in Scripture about slippage:

Therefore we must pay much closer attention to what we have heard, lest we drift away from it (Heb. 2:1).

Uphold my steps in your paths, that my footsteps may not slip (Ps. 17:5, NKJV).

Contend earnestly for the faith which was once for all delivered to the saints (Jude 3, NKJV).

The apostle Paul was able to say that in his ministry he had not shrunk back from declaring the whole counsel of God (Acts 20:27). And the psalmist envisages something much more serious than a slippery slope when he warns against the danger of foundations being destroyed (Ps. 11:3).

All this means that we must approach all change with caution, aware of our sinful and foolish tendency to slide, mindful also of the wisdom of those who have gone before us (e.g. Prov. 22:28).

Another adage is that we should not 'throw out the baby with the bath water'. This also has traction in the business of managing change. There can be a tendency to discard what is valuable and precious with what is dispensable or worthless.

I do not wish to throw out the baby with the bath water with respect to my own Strict Baptist heritage. In many ways it is a good heritage. I had godly role models. I heard Christ-exalting ministry. There were emphases – on the vital need of a personal work of the Holy Spirit and on reverence in worship, for example - that have stayed with me all my life. If in some of these pages we have tended to focus on getting rid of bath water, we must be careful not to throw out the baby with it.

Heart matters

One of the strong emphases of my upbringing was on the importance of 'experimental religion', by which is meant the power of the things of God experienced, known in the heart and soul by the work of the Holy Spirit.

Classically there are three main components in biblical Christianity - doctrine, experience and practice. It seems to me that experience is in its right place in the middle of that trio. Christian experience needs to be anchored in Christian doctrine. Christian practice is at its most potent when it comes from a heart moved by the love of Christ and the deep things of God. Is there a tendency in modern evangelicalism to deduce the practice straight from the doctrine, almost to bypass experience?

In recent years there has been a wonderful resurgence of interest in the great doctrines of the gospel, the doctrines of grace, but is it possible for these to be preached and held in a rather dry, cerebral way? The doctrines of grace are, after all, an intellectually rigorous and satisfying systematic theology. Do we hold the doctrine more in the head than the heart? We rightly have a high view of Scripture, but do we then become satisfied with accurate and clear exegesis as an end in itself? Does preaching, for example, become mostly about presentation, developing the right tools and skills? And do congregations become adept at recognising and appreciating such skills? If so, it will not be surprising if the impact of our preaching is diminished, both in its gospel effectiveness and in its practical application to our lives. Thus we may be in danger of giving assent to the truth, but in reality finding our emotional fulfilment elsewhere.

If indeed we do present an over-intellectualised version of Christianity, what effect will this have on the kind of people we find ourselves addressing? Will our congregations self-select in terms of being middle class, professional and academic?

Preaching is about capturing both minds and hearts. It comes with a prophetic emphasis, 'Thus says the Lord.' It is addressed to people: all kinds of people. It aims at their hearts. One of the strengths of a preacher like William Gadsby was that he was preaching as a working man to working men and women. He was not Bible college trained. His ministry had great impact in Manchester where he became well known throughout the city. It seems strange that Gadsby's followers today, by and large, do not seem to share his radical evangelistic, church-planting passion. Taking our cue from men like Gadsby, we who preach today need to remember that we are not simply preaching a passage or a text or a subject. We are preaching Christ, to people where they are. We are preaching to capture hearts and lives for Christ. In his song at the end of Deuteronomy, Moses says:

> May my teaching drop as the rain, my speech distil as the dew, like gentle rain upon the tender grass, and like showers upon the herb. For I will proclaim the name of the Lord; ascribe greatness to our God (Deut. 32:2-3).

At a Puritan Conference in 1967, Dr Martyn Lloyd-Jones thought that the subject of Sandemanianism was worth considering. In the 1750s, Robert Sandeman (1718-1771) took on the leadership of a movement within the Church of Scotland begun by his father-in-law, John Glas. Its predominant feature was its intellectual view of faith. Saving faith, it said, is 'bare belief of the bare truth'. Regeneration accompanies intellectual assent to the central truths of the Christian faith. No doubt this reflects, as many changing emphases in theology do, the swing of the pendulum. Sandeman was reacting against the undue subjectivism that reigned in certain quarters of eighteenth-century evangelicalism. It is sadly possible for believers to be more taken with their religious experiences than with Christ himself. Faith is thus reduced to little more than religious feeling. However, whilst faith is never only feeling it can never be separated from feeling. In his *Religious Affections*, Jonathan Edwards writes:

> Spiritual understanding ... consists in a sense of the heart, of the supreme beauty and sweetness of the holiness or moral perfection of divine things, together with all that discerning and knowledge of things of religion, that depends upon, and flows from, such a sense ... That sort of knowledge by which a man has a sensible perception of amiableness and loathsomeness, or of sweetness and nauseousness, is not just the same sort of knowledge with that, by which he knows what a triangle is, and what a square is. The one is more speculative knowledge; the other sensible knowledge, in which more than the intellect is concerned; the heart is the proper subject of it, or the soul, as a being that not only beholds, but has inclination, and is pleased or displeased. And yet there is the nature of instruction in it; as he that has perceived the sweet taste of honey, knows much more about it, than he who has only looked at it.

This captures Edwards's main case – the core of true Christianity is in genuine spiritual affections. Again he writes:

> God glorifies himself towards the creatures in two ways: one by appearing to their understanding, and two by communicating himself to their hearts and their rejoicing and delighting in and enjoying the manifestations he makes of himself. God is glorified not only by his glories being seen, but by it being rejoiced in. When those that see it delight in it, God is more glorified than if they only see it, his glory is then received by the whole soul, both by the understanding and by the heart.[45]

Clearly, we need to avoid the dangers of unhealthy introversion and subjectivism. These can be seen in the restless search, found among quite disparate groups of Christians, for extraordinary experiences and spiritual intensity. We also need to beware, however, of the idea that saving faith is simply receiving as true certain propositions about Jesus.

I have strong memories as a boy and young man of being captivated in heart and mind as Christ was preached. Some ministers I heard preach seemed to step into the pulpit from being in the very presence of God. Their faces shone. They exalted Christ. They preached from the heart to the heart. Such preaching had unction. Perhaps today we need to guard against the 'lecture' and the 'presentation' mentality: and, in the desire to communicate, any tendency towards flippancy, entertainment or contrivance. Preaching is, and should be,

45 Jonathan Edwards, *Religious Affections*, Part III Section 4: cited by Michael Haykin, 'Sandemanianism', *Evangelical Times*, September 1998.

truth on fire, person to person, the whole person to the whole person. It is a man doing what Moses did in Numbers 16 – standing between the dead and the living (Num. 16:48). It is expository but not only expository. For the hearer it is an experience, not of emotional manipulation, but of the presence of God in his Word, as the apostle Paul famously writes, 'our gospel came to you not only in word, but also in power and in the Holy Spirit and with full conviction' (1 Thess. 1:5).

Yes, a church with a heart for the lost will be a church that engages in outreach, a church ready to count the cost of removing barriers that stand in the way of reaching the lost. Yet, since matters of the heart are of such significance, it also follows that not all of a church's passion, preaching and programmes will be poured into outreach. The spiritual growth of the flock, the feeding of souls, is also a great work to be done in dependence on the Holy Spirit.

Joy and reverence in worship

Closely linked with both endeavours, is our need earnestly to pray for, and jealously to guard, a real sense of the presence of God in our church life and worship. Jesus said, 'Where two or three are gathered in my name, there am I among them' (Matt. 18:20). What an awesome reality! How it should affect how we behave! What joy and reverence it should bring! If the bath water we seek to be rid of is affectation and hypocrisy, a put-on reverence or joy, the precious living reality we must seek to retain is Christ among his people. This always brings both reverence and joy. How could it result in a sombre gloominess, or an excitable frivolity? One of our older men regularly prays 'for a chapel full of the presence of God'. It is a good prayer.

One aspect of this is our approach to the Lord's Day. Most evangelicals have rightly rejected a legalistic, pharisaical Sabbatarianism. However, are we drifting away from our joyful commitment to celebrate every week the resurrection of the Lord Jesus Christ? The letter to the Hebrews commands us to re-enter the rest of faith in him, and to gather with his people each time that they agree to do so on the Lord's Day and at other times (Heb. 10:24–25).

Distinctive Christian lifestyle

There was a tendency in a previous generation, not only among Strict Baptists, but among evangelicals generally, to have a clear doctrine of separation from the world, and a fairly precise idea of what it looks like on the ground. The Bible is clear on the sanctifying work of the Holy Spirit, and the need for Christians to pursue holiness (e.g. Heb. 12:14). The apostle Paul quotes God speaking to Israel through the prophet Isaiah:

> Come out from among them and be separate, says the Lord. Do not touch what is unclean, And I will receive you (2 Cor. 6:17, NKJV).[46]

Paul adds that it is a priority for New Testament believers to cleanse themselves 'from every defilement of body and spirit' (2 Cor. 7:1). This separation from the world was perhaps over-defined in many areas of life for a previous generation. There was an unwritten list of taboos in terms of places of

---

46 cf. Isa. 52:11.

entertainment, habits, dress and so on. There was a clear emphasis on the importance of example and maintaining a clear witness. The problem with a rule-based approach is that cultural conditions and messages do change over time. This means that the taboos also change, bringing confusion and criticism. True godliness does not flourish in a climate of suspicion and legalism.

In rejecting legalism, however, we need to be careful not to reject biblical distinctiveness, role models and witness. In church life, we must hold before our people the hope and vision of a radical, changed lifestyle motivated by the love of Christ (2 Cor. 5:14–15). The pastoral epistles, especially, show us what true godliness looks like at street level. Inner attitudes of heart produce godly outward actions and behaviour. Churches today have straplines, buzz words, mission statements. Not many of these seem to include godliness. We need to be preaching for godly character, godly lifestyle, godly contentment. Godly people are a good advertisement, they commend God to others. It is very dangerous to the cause of Christ when Christians drift into the world's sliding values (2 Tim. 4:10). Our western worldly culture is marked by self-indulgence and materialism. What if we Christians can scarcely be told apart from our neighbours?

The key is to be found, not in going it alone, but in the new community, the church, the culturally diverse yet united family of the people of God in a local place. Our approach to life today tends to be much more individualistic than in the first century AD. The vision of the New Testament is of shared lives, living out the faith in the body of Christ – corporate, accountable, godly living, distinct from the world.

Conclusion:
'All things for the glory of God'

We can return, as we conclude, to the apostle Paul. He is our prime example of total rigidity about what is fixed – the gospel itself - and of purposeful flexibility where there is genuine freedom of conscience and practice. In fact, as we have seen, Paul could see a real threat to the gospel itself when people insist on being fixed in areas where they ought to be flexible. In a famous passage he exhorts the believers at Corinth:

> So, whether you eat or drink, or whatever you do, do all to the glory of God. Give no offence to Jews or Greeks or to the church of God, just as I try to please everyone in everything I do, not seeking my own advantage: but that of many, that they may be saved. Be imitators of me, as I am of Christ (1 Cor. 10:31 — 11:1).

A gospel heart is beating. Paul wants people of all kinds to be saved. When I want things 'my way' because they are my own preference, or to my advantage, true gospel ambition and advance is impeded. Paul wants the Corinthians to lay down that burden - for burden it is. He wants them rather to be motivated by a double desire – 'to do all to the glory of

God', and at the same time 'to please everyone in everything I do'. Biblically, these two things are not essentially conflicted. We must be willing to do anything, change anything that may be changed, if only we can bring people the glorious message of free salvation in Jesus Christ. We must cross the necessary pain thresholds to remove stumbling blocks in the way of this great message being heard and received. This is the servant-heart which Christ himself exhibited with such supreme grace. And the apostle Paul was able to say, 'be imitators of me, as I am of Christ'.

In this great enterprise, the church is God's change agent to the world. The value-system and lifestyle of the world is challenged, turned upside down, as the message of the gospel is brought to it. It is the world's only hope. If, in the process, the church herself needs to change, that change needs to be faced, managed and effected to the glory of God. This can be done with complete confidence in the sufficiency of the Word of God. As this Word is taught and exemplified, gospel change will follow.

Godly change is not therefore about reacting to the past or reflecting current trends and fashions. It is about working for a future that is more closely modelled on the Word of God and the pattern of Jesus Christ. It is about change not only at an institutional but also at a personal level. The key to it all must be the ministry of the Word of God in the congregation - the preaching of the Bible by the power and help of the Holy Spirit.

By sharing our journey as a church in these pages, my hope is that our story might be of some help to others in local church contexts. But there is great comfort and liberty in the thought that, in the end, it is not all down to us. For all that has been wanting on our watch and in our efforts, we cast ourselves on the mercy of God. Whatever has been good in our bumpy course of change has been entirely of his grace. To God be the glory!

Appendix:

A Little Bit of History

Baptist origins in Coventry can be traced back as early as 1652. We know that a chapel was erected in 1724 in Jordan Well. Its first pastor was John Brine (1726-1729). John Butterworth was pastor from 1753 to 1803. In 1753, when the population of Coventry was 12,000, the church had 90 members. In 1793, as a result of growth in numbers, the church moved to a new chapel in Cow Lane, where, in that same year, William Gadsby was baptised.[47] Francis Franklin came to Cow Lane as an assistant pastor in 1799 and succeeded John Butterworth in 1803. Franklin opposed Gadsby and this had the effect of causing a split in 1820, when a number left Cow Lane chapel. They opened a house for worship and invited Gadsby and others to preach there. In 1830 the services were held in a hired building, but after a while these were discontinued, and they travelled to Bedworth for their services.

---

47 The compiler of *Gadsby's Selection of Hymns* (1838) referred to above, and author of several hymns still sung today including perhaps most famously, 'Immortal honours rest on Jesus' head' (*Gadsby's* 667).

The church that has been the subject of these pages is older than the chapel building itself. About the year 1849 one of these people began a meeting on Sunday afternoons in his home in Coventry. The response was encouraging and Mr Barber, a wholesale grocer, provided a meeting room in his yard, capable of seating a hundred people. On 31 October 1852 a church was formed. This is the group who built the chapel, Rehoboth. The present church and congregation is in direct continuation and the statement of faith in its trust document is still in place. Benjamin Poole gives an account of how the chapel came to be built in 1857:

> The congregation to which the chapel belongs, sprung from a small number of persons of the Particular Baptist persuasion, but adhering more tenaciously to, or promulgating more emphatically, the Calvinistic doctrine than other Baptists in Coventry were supposed to do. They met for some years in a room upon the premises of one of their members ... and in their first attempt to obtain a site for the erection of a place of worship, a refusal to sell the land for the building of a dissenting chapel, compelled them to seek elsewhere for a site, which they ultimately found where their building now stands, and which they obtained without strife about the matter; where they found room enough for their then existing requirements, and to multiply or be fruitful hereafter. Hence the application to their own case, of a passage in the life of the patriarch Isaac, during his journeyings in the valley of Gerar, and his dispute with the herdsmen there about the digging of the wells, Genesis 26.22.[48]

48 Benjamin Poole, *History and Antiquities of Coventry* (Smith and Taunton, 1863).

So the chapel was named Rehoboth ('The Lord has made room for us'), and opened on Christmas Day 1857, John Kershaw preaching from the text, 'And thou shalt call his name Jesus, for he shall save his people from their sins' (Matt. 1:21).

It is interesting to reflect on the various changes that have occurred in Baptist life in the last 360 or so years. Somehow or other that change has been managed and there is still a witness to the unchanging truth of the gospel in Coventry today. There is still an unashamed testimony to the gospel of God's free and sovereign grace. It has been a privilege to be involved in a small fraction of its history.

Acknowledgements

Without the encouragement of family and friends I doubt this book would have been written. Throughout my ministry I have been blessed with the prayerful and loving support of godly men and women – especially the elders, deacons and church members of what is now Hillfields Church Coventry. You have borne with my foibles and encouraged me constantly by your love for Christ and his great gospel of grace.

Two men from the early years I would particularly like to mention, David Adams and Philip Stone, both now with the Lord, who so graciously adapted to the new pastor who began his ministry at Rehoboth Chapel in 1985. From more recent years James Young stands out - a truly gospel-hearted fellow-worker. Thank you, James, for your patience with me when I have been slow to follow through on gospel-driven change.

I have complete confidence that no one else in the church family will mind in the least when I say that, in terms of personal fellowship, encouragement and loyal support one brother is of 'head and shoulders' stature. Peter Cordle has been a faithful friend and mentor to me throughout the whole journey mapped out in this book. We have stood together in the battles, shared the joys and the heartaches. Thank you, Peter.

Then of course there is my family – my dear wife, Hazel, and my three children and their families. Dan, Becky and Tim have grown up bearing the peculiar burden of being PKs (pastor's kids), but I think they've learned good people skills as a result. All three have read my manuscript, made helpful comments on it, and spurred me on to write. They, their spouses and now their children, continue to inspire me by their desire to follow Jesus.

A special joy in the production of this book has been the editorial guidance and skill of Jim Sayers who has shown an intuitive grasp both of our story itself and the challenges it raises for churches and Christians today. Our sessions on Zoom have been rich times of sharing.

Also by Grace Publications

Pure Church

Edited by David Skull, Andrew King & Jim Sayers

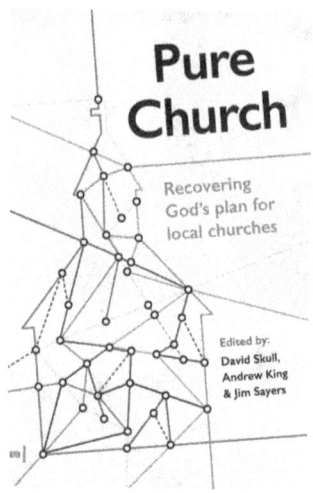

Recently there has been a concern for the health of gospel churches. But very often that concern comes down to the introduction of a few new items to the church agenda.

This book's vision is that the whole way a church should be formed should work for the health of all its members. It is a church with an intentional mindset. It is a church where all the dots are joined up.

'This is exactly what Christianity needs, but doesn't know it.'
Jonathan Leeman

Available to buy from gracepublications.co.uk